The UNIVERSAL *Library*

	UL		UL
THE DANCE OF LIFE *Havelock Ellis*	2	THE AMERICAN PRESIDENCY *Laski*	40
THE GOOD SOCIETY *Walter Lippmann*	3	STALIN *Leon Trotsky*	41
THE LATE GEORGE APLEY *Marquand*	4	U.S. GRANT AND THE AMERICAN	
MAN AND HIS GODS *Homer Smith*	5	MILITARY TRADITION *Bruce Catton*	42
THE MEASURE OF MAN *J. W. Krutch*	6	THE VANISHING HERO *Sean O'Faolain*	43
MELBOURNE *Lord David Cecil*	7	KARL MARX: THE RED PRUSSIAN	
OSCAR WILDE *Hesketh Pearson*	8	*Leopold Schwarzschild*	44
THE PURITAN OLIGARCHY		DECLINE AND FALL *Evelyn Waugh*	45
Thomas Wertenbaker	9	MODERN WOMAN: THE LOST SEX	
QUACKERY IN THE PUBLIC SCHOOLS		*Lundberg and Farnham*	46
Albert Lynd	10	ANDREW JACKSON: BORDER CAPTAIN	
REVEILLE IN WASHINGTON *Leech*	11	*Marquis James*	47
THE WEB AND THE ROCK *Thomas Wolfe*	12	THE HORSE'S MOUTH *Joyce Cary*	48
THE IDES OF MARCH *Thornton Wilder*	13	GREEN MANSIONS *W. H. Hudson*	49
NOBLE ESSENCES *Sir Osbert Sitwell*	14	MYTHS OF THE WORLD *Padraic Colum*	50
WHY WAS LINCOLN MURDERED?		THE OWL IN THE ATTIC *Thurber*	51
Otto Eisenschiml	15	MRS. EDDY *Edwin F. Dakin*	52
YOU CAN'T GO HOME AGAIN *Wolfe*	16	OCCUPATION: WRITER *Robert Graves*	53
THE SHOCK OF RECOGNITION		THE TASTEMAKERS *Russell Lynes*	54
edited by *Edmund Wilson*		WITH NAPOLEON IN RUSSIA	
(Vol. I—The 19th Century)	17	*Armand de Caulaincourt*	55
(Vol. II—The 20th Century)	18	COMEDIES OF OSCAR WILDE	56
HERCULES, MY SHIPMATE *Robert Graves*	19	MADAME BOVARY *Gustave Flaubert*	57
THE SELECTED LETTERS OF LORD BYRON		PRIDE AND PREJUDICE *Jane Austen*	58
edited by *Jacques Barzun*	20	NINE PLAYS OF CHEKOV	59
IRISH FOLK STORIES AND FAIRY TALES		MCSORLEY'S WONDERFUL SALOON	
William Butler Yeats	21	*Joseph Mitchell*	60
SOUTH WIND *Norman Douglas*	22	THE ART OF LOVE *Ovid*	61
THE UPROOTED *Oscar Handlin*	23	NIJINSKY *Romola Nijinsky*	62
JOHN ADAMS AND THE AMERICAN REVO-		CRIME AND PUNISHMENT *Dostoevsky*	63
LUTION *Catherine Drinker Bowen*	24	MISTER JELLY ROLL *Alan Lomax*	64
THE LONGHORNS *J. Frank Dobie*	25	THE TOWN AND THE CITY *Jack Kerouac*	65
THE LIFE AND TIMES OF LUCREZIA BORGIA		50 POEMS *e. e. cummings*	66
Maria Bellonci	26	HERSELF SURPRISED *Joyce Cary*	67
THE STORY OF MY LIFE		JANE AUSTEN *Elizabeth Jenkins*	68
Clarence Darrow	27	MIDDLE-AGED MAN ON THE FLYING	
THE WORLD OF ALDOUS HUXLEY		TRAPEZE *James Thurber*	69
edited by *Charles J. Rolo*	28	SELECTED WRITINGS OF FRANK LLOYD	
THE GREAT PLAINS *Walter Prescott Webb*	29	WRIGHT edited by *F. Gutheim*	70
AN AMERICAN DOCTOR'S ODYSSEY		EYEWITNESS *Eisenschiml & Newman*	71
Victor Heiser	30	MY LIFE *Leon Trotsky*	72
FOUR PLAYS BY IBSEN	31	A POCKETFUL OF WRY *McGinley*	73
SHORTER NOVELS OF HERMAN MELVILLE	32	MARCH OF THE IRON MEN *Burlingame*	74
THE STAR-GAZER *Zsolt de Harsanyi*	33	EDITOR TO AUTHOR *Perkins · Wheelock*	75
FREUD AND HIS TIME *Fritz Wittels*	34	SPEAK, MEMORY *Vladimir Nabokov*	76
PRIMITIVE RELIGION *Robert H. Lowie*	35	LET YOUR MIND ALONE *Thurber*	77
MAUPASSANT: A LION IN THE PATH		DISRAELI *Hesketh Pearson*	78
Francis Steegmuller	36	ROOSEVELT & HOPKINS *Sherwood*	79
THE GREEN CROW *Sean O'Casey*	37	TO BE A PILGRIM *Joyce Cary*	80
11 PLAYS OF THE GREEK DRAMATISTS —		CHURCHILL: THE ERA AND THE MAN	
Aeschylus, Sophocles, Euripides and		*Virginia Cowles*	81
Aristophanes	38	D. H. LAWRENCE: A BASIC STUDY OF	
SELECTED NOVELS OF HENRY JAMES	39	HIS IDEAS *Mary Freeman*	82

PHYLLIS McGINLEY

is one of America's most successful writers of light verse — light only in the sense that they are easy and enjoyable to read. Miss McGinley's poems have always had that modicum of truth, that substance of wit and feeling which reveal the intrinsic quality of her thoughts and craftsmanship. Born in Ontario, Oregon, Miss McGinley started writing verse at the age of six. Her first book of poems, On the Contrary, was published in 1934. In 1944 Miss McGinley made her debut as a children's writer with The Horse Who Lived Upstairs. Many others followed. In 1954 Miss McGinley secured a place on the best seller list for a long period with her engaging volume of poems, The Love Letters of Phyllis McGinley. In 1955 Miss McGinley was elected to the National Academy of Arts and Letters.

This present volume of poems, A Pocketful of Wry, is a new, revised edition of the original collection.

PHYLLIS McGINLEY

A Pocketful of Wry

NEWLY REVISED EDITION

The Universal Library

GROSSET & DUNLAP

NEW YORK

I. PUBLIC FACES

MILLENNIUM   3

ADVICE TO A TOT ABOUT TO LEARN THE ALPHABET   5

ODE TO THE END OF SUMMER   7

BALLAD OF THE PREELECTION VOTE   9

COMPLAINT TO THE AMERICAN MEDICAL ASSOCIATION   11

DEATH WITH SOUND EFFECTS   14

PRIMARY EDUCATION   16

STAR-SPANGLED ODE   18

THE GOOD CITIZEN   22

LESS INFORMATION, PLEASE   23

HANDS ACROSS THE HEADLINES   25

PUBLIC JOURNAL   27

PROGRESS   30

MESSAGE FOUND IN A BOTTLE   31

THE OUTCAST   33

THE GREAT ENIGMA   35

MEMORANDUM FOR A LYNCHING   37

LESSON FOR LADIES   39

SONG AGAINST SWEETNESS AND LIGHT   41

MESSAGE FROM MARS   43

A MODEL FOR MUDDLERS   45

BALLAD OF FINE DAYS   47

TACTICS FOR OFFENSE   48

THE WEB   50

POOR TIMING   51

PETITION TO THE POSTMASTER-GENERAL   53

THE PROGRESS OF DICTATORSHIP   55

GO ON, YOU SCINTILLATE   56

BALLAD OF THE LORD AND COLUMBUS   58

II. ON THE TOWN

DIRGE OVER A POT OF PATE DE FOIE GRAS   65

INCIDENT ON MADISON AVENUE   67

SALE TODAY   69

CALENDAR FOR NEW YORKERS   70

STILL LIFE   72

LAMENT   73

LETTER TO THE SIXTH AVENUE ASSOCIATION   75

COUNTRY WEEK END, RAINY   77

REBUKE TO SCHIAPARELLI   79

MUSINGS ABOARD THE STAMFORD LOCAL   82

ADMONITION IN JANUARY   83

MONOLOGUE IN A PET SHOP   85

III. PRIVATE AND PERSONAL

LAMENT FOR A WAVERING VIEWPOINT   89

WHY, SOME OF MY BEST FRIENDS ARE WOMEN!   91

ODE TO THE BATH   93

NURSERY RHYME   96

SHORT HISTORY OF COOKS   97

APOLOGY FOR HUSBANDS   99

COMEUPPANCE FOR A PROGENY   101

SOLD: TO THE LADY IN THE GREEN HAT   103

MUCH ADO ABOUT NOTHING   105

ELEGY FROM A COUNTRY DOORYARD   107

SONG FOR AN ENGRAVED INVITATION   109

A HOBBY A DAY KEEPS THE DOLDRUMS AWAY   111

MILLINERY MEMO   113

TWELFTH NIGHT   114

WELL, WELL, CHARLIE'S IN TOWN   115

INVENTORS, KEEP AWAY FROM MY DOOR   117

THE FEMALE OF THE SPECIES IS HARDIER THAN THE MALE   119

LINES FROM A PORCH SWING   121

TRAVEL SONG WITH A FAINT HINT OF NOSTALGIA   122

THE CHOSEN PEOPLE   124

THE LASS WITH THE MONDAY AIR   126

SONG FOR A BRAND-NEW HOUSE   128

PLEASE LOCK THE HARDWARE STORE   130

NOTES FOR A SOUTHERN ROAD MAP   132

VERSES FOR A GREETING CARD   134

HUMBLESSE OBLIGE   135

IV. A TROUBLED POOL

NOTES FOR AN ANTHROPOLOGIST   139

OLD RHYME   141

THE OLD WOMAN WITH FOUR SONS   142

ADDRESS TO THE YOUNGER GENERATION   143

ON EVERY FRONT   145

YOUNG MAN WITH AN HEIR   147

PORTRAIT   149

MR. BROWNING REVISES—1940   151

INTIMATIONS OF MORTALITY   152

I

PUBLIC FACES

Millennium

Some day,
Some blank, odd, pallid, immemorial day,
Some curious Monday,
Some Tuesday, Wednesday, Thursday, Friday, Saturday,
Or even Sunday,
I shall arise dishevelled and a gaper,
To scan the paper
And stare thereon, thumb through, search it for clues,
Peruse and re-peruse,
And find no news.

Nothing to heat the blood or race the pulse,
Nothing at all—
No six-inch headlines screaming a war's results
Or a city's fall.
No threats, no bombs, no air-raids, no alarms,
No feats of arms,
No foe at any gate,
No politics, no shouting candidate;
Nothing exclusive, not a censored phrase,
No Scoops, no Exposés;
No crisis either foreign or domestic,
Nothing wild, urgent, imminent or drastic
Happening on the earth.

Only reports of weather and the birth
Of triplets to a lioness at the Zoo,
(Printed within a box)
And yesterday's sermons seeming scarcely new
And something about the White-or-Sundry-Sox;

3

An actress married or divorced or dead,
Who led
The golfing in some tournament or other.

Oh, I shall smother
In ennui, I shall nod and yawn
And fling the dull sheets down upon the lawn,
Bored near to death by what they have to say
On that strange, beautiful day.

Advice to a Tot About to Learn the Alphabet

Consider, child. Be prudent.
  Rash infant, not so fast!
Oh, stay, my dimpled student,
  Unlettered to the last.
Unless you leap before you look,
  Your fate will be a trite one.
For first you'll learn to read a book
  And then you'll want to write one.
The Pulitzers, the Guggenheims,
  Will rank you with the winners.
You'll print a play, compose some rhymes,
And be reviewed in the Sunday *Times*
And get invited for your crimes
  To Literary Dinners.

You'll be a Guest of Honor on a small, gold chair,
Consuming filet mignon with a literary air.
You'll grace the Speakers' Table, with authors flanked about,
For the Culture Groups will get you if you don't watch out.

Between the lions and parrots,
  Behind the potted shrubs,
You'll munch on peas and carrots
  And talk to Women's Clubs.
'Mid microphones and ferny fronds
  You'll raise your cultured voice
So dowagers in diamonds
  Can listen and rejoice,
So folk who take their authors neat
  Can boast they lingered nigh one,

5

And from a paid, impartial seat
Can gaze upon you while you eat
And twitter that your book was *sweet,*
   But never, never buy one.

Oh, princes thrive on caviar, the poor on whey and curds,
And politicians, I infer, must eat their windy words.
It's crusts that feed the virtuous, it's cake that comforts sinners,
But writers live on bread and praise at Literary Dinners.

So shun this vain utensil
   Before it is too late.
Throw down the bitten pencil,
   Discard the perilous slate,
Else soon you'll start to scribble verse
   And then you'll write a tome,
And so you'll go from bad to worse
   And never dine at home.
You'll buy yourself an opera hat
   And learn to speak with unction
And end a Guest of Honor at
   A Literary Function.

You'll be a Guest of Honor on a hard, gold chair,
With your name upon the menu just below the bill of fare,
And you'll sing for your supper while the lesser authors pout,
For the Culture Clubs will get you if you don't watch out.

Ode to the End of Summer

Summer, adieu.
            Adieu, gregarious season.
Goodbye, 'revoir, farewell.
Now day comes late; now chillier blows the breeze on
Forsaken beach and boarded-up hotel.
Now wild geese fly together in thin lines
And Tourist Homes take down their lettered signs.

It fades—this green, this lavish interval,
This time of flowers and fruits,
Of melon ripe along the orchard wall,
Of sun and sails and wrinkled linen suits;
Time when the world seems rather plus than minus
And pollen tickles the allergic sinus.

Now fugitives to farm and shore and highland
Cancel their brief escape.
The Ferris wheel is quiet at Coney Island
And quaintness trades no longer on the Cape;
While meek-eyed parents hasten down the ramps
To greet their offspring, terrible from camps.

Turn up the steam. The year is growing older.
The maple boughs are red.
Summer, farewell. Farewell the sunburnt shoulder,
Farewell the peasant kerchief on the head.
Farewell the thunderstorm, complete with lightning,
And the white shoe that ever needeth whitening.

Farewell, vacation friendships, sweet but tenuous.
Ditto to slacks and shorts.

7

Farewell, O strange compulsion to be strenuous
Which sends us forth to death on tennis courts.
Farewell, Mosquito, horror of our nights;
Clambakes, iced tea, and transatlantic flights.

The zinnia withers, mortal as the tulip.
Now from the dripping glass
I'll sip no more the amateur mint julep
Nor dine al fresco on the alien grass;
Nor scale the height nor breast the truculent billow
Nor lay my head on any weekend pillow.

Unstintingly I yield myself to Autumn
And Equinoctial sloth.
I hide my swim suit in the bureau's bottom
Nor fear the fury of the after-moth.
Forswearing porch and pool and beetled garden,
My heart shall rest, my arteries shall harden.

Welcome, kind Fall, and every month with "r" in
Whereto my mind is bent.
Come, sedentary season that I star in,
O fire-lit Winter of my deep content!
Amid the snow, the sleet, the blizzard's raw gust,
I shall be cozier than I was in August.

Safe from the picnic sleeps the unlittered dell.
The last Good Humor sounds its final bell,
And all is silence.
                    Summer, farewell, farewell.

Ballad of the Preëlection Vote

November's gale already
　　Disturbs the summer dust.
The breezes whirl and eddy
　　With straws in every gust,
With straws in every gust, tra-la,
　　And polls in every section,
Designed to show
How winds can blow
　　And eke in whose direction.

Now, terrible and tireless,
　　The ballots fall like hail.
They search us out by wireless,
　　They clog the morning mail.
No candidate too pallid,
　　No issue too remote,
But it can snare
A questionnaire
　　To analyze our vote.

And shore to rocky shore, now,
　　Stirring the nation's pulse,
Begins the mighty war, now,
　　Of Differing Results.
The leaders shout a warning,
　　The experts spin their arts.
From South and North
They Gallup forth
　　With averages and charts.

And some by slogans mystic
  Rouse countryside and town
To challenge the statistic
  Or cry the verdict down;
But no one hurries faster
  To point us out a flaw
Than the nominee
Who seems to be
  The turkey in the straw.

Complaint to the American Medical Association

(CONCERNING THEIR MEMBERS' UNFAIR MONOPOLY OF BEST-SELLING
AUTOBIOGRAPHIES AND OTHER FICTION)

Of all God's creatures here below
   Whose feats confound the skeptic
I most admire the Medico,
   That hero antiseptic.
He has my heart, he has my hand,
   He has my utmost loyalties.
(He also has my tonsils and
   A lien on my royalties.)
For from the time he doth begin
His sacred tryst with medicine,
How noble, he! How never-tiring!
Not rain, nor heat, nor maids admiring,
Nor bills unpaid, nor farmers' hounds
Can stay him from his sleepless rounds.
More fleet than winners of the Bendix,
He hastens to the burst appendix,
Or breasts the blizzard cold and shivery
To make some rural free delivery.

Or if to ampler orbits whirled
   (As fate will sometimes toss us),
How he bestrides this narrow world,
   A medical Colossus!
Perhaps, his kit upon his back,
   He dares the jungle thickets,
Intent upon the fevered track
   Of yaws or mumps or rickets.

11

The chum of kings, the friend of presidents,
He makes the earth his private residence;
One day prescribing pills and pickups
To cure an emperor of hiccups,
The next in stricken cities stranded,
Combatting scourges single-handed,
At peril of life, at risk of limb.
Yet do such deeds suffice for him?
No, no. In secret all the while
He's sought a Literary Style.

The pen (so springs the constant hope
    Of all devout physicians)
Is mightier than the stethoscope
    And runs to more editions.
So while he's waged bacillic wars,
    Or sewed a clever suture,
His mind has hummed with metaphors
    Laid up against the future.
Amid the knives and sterile gauzes
He's dreamt of modifying clauses,
And never gone to bed so late
His diary wasn't up to date,
As if he'd sworn an oath to follow
Both Harper Brothers and Apollo.
Oh, more than Einstein, more than Edison
I do admire the man of Medison.
He has my hand, he has my note,
He has those X-rays of my throat,
But is it fair he should lay claim to
The overcrowded writing game, too?

I eye askance those dubious laurels.
Where are his ethics? Where his morals?
In what brave school did he matriculate
That he should be so damned articulate?
And where's the seal to show his betters
He's certified a Man of Letters?

Professional sirs, I gravely doubt,
  In any really nice sense,
Your boys should practice thus without
  Their literary license.

Death With Sound Effects

VERSES COMPOSED UPON HEARING THAT SCIENTISTS ARE RECORDING THE
MATING CALLS OF MOSQUITOES AND PLAN TO USE THEM TO LURE THE
INSECTS TO THEIR DOWNFALL

When summer's warm upon the breeze
   And evening shrouds the glens,
Oh, pity poor Anopheles
   And Culex Pipiens,
Whom Science, on deliberate vote,
Has destined for a *Liebestod*.

The mists will fall, the moon will rise,
   Darkness the daylight veto.
Then forward to his strange demise
   Will race the blithe mosquito,
Antennae turned to catch the tender
Accents of the female gender.

From duty will he turn away
   To bear an ardent torch.
He'll leave his work and leave his play
   On patio or porch,
Desert the foray intramural,
The city roof, the terrace rural,
The chosen grasses, moist and deep,
The chamber dedicate to sleep,
The bright, the unscreened living room,
And hurry off to meet his doom—
Yea, quit, no matter how it rankles,

His job on easy arms and ankles.
Foregoing much, forgetting all,
    Save love or matrimony,
He'll fly—to find that mating call
    A trick, a trap, a phony,
And come to grief with no defense,
The victim of his sentiments.

For thus, weighed down by nature's fetters,
The lower orders ape their betters.

Primary Education

"Pupils to Learn Tolerance Here Twice a Month."—Headline in the *Herald Tribune*.

By hook, by crook, by hair of head,
   By scruff of neck and seat of pants,
Our stubborn infants shall be led
   Along the paths of tolerance.

As bends the twig, thus grows the el-em;
   As twists the thread, the spool unwinds;
So, twice a month, we're bound to sell 'em
   The doctrine of Impartial Minds.

Tagged, labelled, catalogued, and graded,
   Sitting submissive in a queue,
Fortnightly they shall be persuaded
   To entertain the Larger View—

To stretch their hands across the ocean;
   To open up their childish hearts
And love their neighbor with devotion,
   As per the diagrams and charts;

To call the foreigner their brother
   (Unless by chance he should indorse
Some heretic opinion other
   Than that included in the Course).

By rote, by rule, by text and primer,
　By maps and slides and lectures read,
We'll see that Truth is set to simmer
　In every tot's intolerant head.

Or so believes the Board of Ed.

Star-Spangled Ode

(FOR PATRIOTIC OCCASIONS)

My country, 'tis to thee and all thy ways
I lift my harp in praise.
Land of tall forests, hills, lakes, seas, and valleys
(The Pilgrims' pride and likewise the O'Malleys'),
Of balmy climes and climates somewhat horrider;
Land of Vermont and Maine and also Florider;
Haven to heroes from oppression fleeting
(Viz.: Kosciusko, Thomas Mann, and Erika);
Country of canyons, corn, and central heating,
 Of thee I sing, America!

While statesmen fume and bicker in thy name,
 Thunder upon the Left or damn the Tories,
My task shall be, unblushing, to proclaim
 Thy singular, matchless, and immoderate glories.

> *Hail, Columbia, happy spot,*
> *Gem of a double ocean.*
> *Here I, embattled patriot,*
> *Publish my stout devotion.*

Hail, birthplace of my Gramp.
 Hail customs, monuments, cities, paths, and byways;
Each garden, farm, park, house, and tourist camp,
 And every trailer on your teeming highways.
Hail, land that loved the French and fought the Hessian,
 That dreamed of unearned riches, like Aladdin;
Place of the Uplift, and the graphed Recession,
 Charlie McCarthy, and Bernarr Macfadden;

That in your ample bosom can enclose
Pikes Peak and Billy Rose,
New England lilacs fragrant where you pass,
And the gold poppy in the Western grass.

For good or ill, this is my chosen nation,
　　Home of Joe Louis and the D.A.R.,
Fairs, floods, the Federal Investigation,
　　And the used car;
Cape Cod, the Coca-Cola, Mount Rainier,
　　The Swanee River and the River Bronx,
The Dies Committee and the roasting ear,
　　And Scottish songs in swing time at the On'x;
Of rocking chairs on country porches rocking,
And the slim leg in the superlative stocking.

All these do I rejoice in with rejoicing:
　　Jones Beach, blueberry pie, and mocking birds,
And Mrs. Doctor Mayo, sweetly voicing
　　American Motherhood's authentic words;
And footballs in October attitudes,
And Automats, and packaged breakfast foods.
Now more and evermore
Dear to my heart is this, my native shore,
Where Liberty lingers still, and even Hope
Unvanquished dwells;
Where dentists ply their trade, and there is soap—
Soap, and hot waters steaming, in hotels.
Where none so humble or his lot so low
But in his house there blares the Radio.

　　　　Oh, beautiful for spacious skies
　　　　　And waving fields of grain,

19

> For everything a buyer buys
> Embalmed in Cellophane.
> America, America,
> I call each prospect good,
> From Maryland
> To the Goldwyn strand
> Of shining Hollywood.

What do we lack that other nations boast of?
  What splendor or what plague?
Unanimous Italy may make the most of
  Her Duce. We have Hague.
As favorably our plains and mountains size up;
  Our suns are brighter and our snows as chill,
And more profusely do our billboards rise up
  On every templed hill.
And if, beneath the tread of iron heels,
Our earth less sickly reels,
  Where are the armies valianter than these—
Our troops of marching boys assembling yet,
Lads without uniform or bayonet,
  Who come to grips with trees?
And we have Donald Duck and Passamaquoddy,
And more laws than *anybody*.

EPILOGUE

Now dies upon my ear
  The eagle screaming and the hollow cheer,
The politician's loud and public tone,
And the La Follette calling to its own.
Only I hear

20

Above the din, the clamor, the stone-flinging,
Freedom, yet faintly ringing.

And by the dawn's dim light I see you stand,
O indestructible land,
Swaggering still, and binding up your hurts,
    Building your towers, digging impossible ditches;
Your leaders clad in ordinary shirts,
    Your Kennedy clinging to his common britches.
So that I cry, secure within your gates,
O.K., United States.

The Good Citizen

"Need for New Hats Chief Reason Women Apply for Jury Duty."
—Headline in the *Herald Tribune*.

When lovely woman sits on jury
  Amid a panel of her peers,
What trumpet call, what civic fury,
  Has brought her to these hemispheres?

Was it her conscience, mutely seeking
  The cozy place where she was at?
Was it the midnight voices speaking
  In tones of Carrie Chapman Catt?

Did duty nag? Did Suffrage nail her?
  The thought's erroneous, though sweet.
It was a red and ribboned sailor
  That led her to the judgment seat.

And though this ground is grave and holy,
  She has no fear thereon to tread,
Content to take the verdict solely
  Upon her head.

Less Information, Please

I remember, I remember, the days of long ago
When soothing to the simple ear remained the radio,
When, safe from pastimes mental
  Or knowledgeable cracks,
To music incidental
  A lady could relax—
Could pull the easy chair down
And snugly let her hair down
And shut the door devoutly
  On predatory facts.
But what pedantic company the witty wireless is, now!
For turn a knob or twist a dial, you get a little Quiz, now.

The ether is littered with learning.
  The experts have cornered the air.
On thousands of stations
They're quoting quotations
  Or bearding the Bard in his lair.
Farewell to the strains, now,
  Of murmurous waltzes.
They're teasing our brains, now,
  With Trueses and Falses.
And whether it's lotions
Or alkaline potions
  Or girdles or gum that they're selling,
With riddles and sly cues
They're testing our I.Q.'s
  Or beating us down on our spelling.

I remember, I remember, the parties that I went to
When gay were those unlettered games which busily we bent to.

Then less than any bubble
  Seemed matters erudite.
With double and redouble
  We sped the festive night.
Oh, Culbertson was God, then,
And seldom did we nod, then,
With dummies to finesse through
  And trumps for our delight.
But grimmer grow the evenings since hostesses expect you all
To gather in the drawing room for doings intellectual.

It's "Mention the source of this Proverb,"
  Or "Name me that Biblical War."
With sprightly endeavor
They bid you be clever
  And solve them—well, three out of four.
No rest for digestions,
  No dancing for dancers!
They ply you with questions
  And plague you for answers.
Now lovers and loafahs
Are lured from their sofas
  To list the Herculean Labors,
While glamour girls pant
To be Oscar Levant
  Or the lads to out-Kieran their neighbors.

So I'm hastening tomorrow for a dim, enchanted shore on
Which there ain't no Information and the natives love a moron;
Ship me somewheres east of Suez where the something's like
    the worst—
Wait a minute! Sure—that's Kipling. And I think I got it first!

24

Hands Across the Headlines

"Our activities seldom bring us together, but we both read *The New York Times*."—Norma Shearer and Virginia Gildersleeve, as quoted in a *Times* testimonial.

Said Barnard's Dean to the Films' First Lady,
"A Scholar's retreat is green and shady,
And since I dwell in this verdant grotto,
Our roads don't cross as they really ought to.
I shun the Kliegs and I seldom rove
In the moonlit depths of the Cocoanut Grove,
While most infrequently I appear
To pose for the Press at a World Premeer.
At Mr. Grauman's astounding portal,
The print of my foot is not immortal,
For I bide at home and I keep my school
And I don't own even one swimming pool.
But wheresoever the future finds us,
It's nice to know there's a tie that binds us—
That over our coffee we both peruse
Identical puns in the Book Reviews,
And no matter how far our pathway varies,
We're reading the same Obituaries."

Said the Films' First Lady to Barnard's Dean,
"I know quite thoroughly what you mean.
For the miles are many, the distance wide,
'Twixt Beverly Hills and Morningside.
I do not listen with mild forbearance
To lamentations of baffled parents,
Or scribble tentative lists of names
For Honor Awards or the Attic Games,

Or teach the Freshman her first allegiance,
Or banquet yearly with Boards of Regents,
And I don't get up near Columbia much—
Still, it is a comfort to keep in touch,
To know our spirits are held in tether
By common reports on War and Weather,
That our eyes both gleam with a similar glint
As we browse through the News That's Fit to Print.
Oh, isn't it fine how our minds agree?"
Said Norma S. to Virginia G.

Public Journal

VERSES INSPIRED BY A DAY SPENT IN COMMUNION WITH THE BRIGHT
YOUNG MEN OF ENGLISH VERSE

> *Christopher Isherwood, Stephen Spender,*
> *Auden and L. MacNeice—*
> *I can't come along on an all-night bender,*
> *But I'll have a quick one with you.*

It is four in the afternoon. Time still for a poem,
A poem not topical, wholly, or romantic, or metaphysic,
But fetched from the grab-bag of my mind and gaudy with
Symbol, slogan, quotation, and even music.
And many a Marxian maxim and many allusions
To a daft system and a world-disorder.
I will mention machines and the eight hour day and
Czecho-Slovakia and the invaded border.

I will speak of love and I will do it slyly,
Unloosing the sacred girdle with a tired air,
Taking particular pains to notice the elastic garters
And the literal underwear.

I will put learning into my poem, for I acquired learning
At Cambridge or Oxford, it does not matter which.
But I'll freshen it up with slang which I got by ear,
Though it may sound a little off pitch.
And I'll be casual with rhymes for that is the trend,
Fashionable as the black hat of Anthony Eden.
I may put them at the middle of the stanza instead of the end,
For really amazing effect.

27

Or perhaps I'll find that assonance heightens the meaning better.
Yes, definitely, I prefer the latter.

Well, it will be sport, writing my private hates
And my personal credo.
I must bring in how I went to Spain on a holiday,
And how cold it was in Toledo.
There was a bootblack, too, in Madrid,
Who gave my shoes a burnish.
He told me something important which I cannot repeat,
For though I understand Spain, I do not understand Spanish.

I'll recall autumn weather in Birmingham,
Drearier than Boston.
And the pump-attendant there who sold me stormy petrol
For my thirsting Austin.

I will put tarts into my poem, and tenement people,
The poor but not the meek;
And pieces of popular songs for a hint of nostalgia,
And bits of Greek.

I shall be tough and ardent and angry-eyed,
Aware that the world is dying, gasping, its face grown pallid;
But quick to embalm it in language as an aspic
Enfolds the chicken salad.

Now it is five o'clock. The poem is finished
Like Poland, like the upper classes, like Sunday's roast.
I must straighten my waistcoat and see that it goes straight out
By the evening post.

28

For what is left for us? Only
The stanza a day,
And the American royalties, and an inherited income,
To keep the wolf at bay.

Progress

"Scientists declare grass contains more vitamins than all other fruits and vegetables put together."—News item in the *Times*.

Nebuchadnezzar, snug in Hell,
  But panting still in that fervid clime,
Read the papers and sighed, "How dull
  To have been a prophet before one's time!

"I ranged the meadows beside the cattle,
  I fed on the fields to atone my sins,
And no one knew I had found a subtle
  Method of getting my vitamins."

"Had I been born to a later people,"
  Cried Babylon's King, "Alack, alas,
How many an eager and lean disciple
  Had followed me out to the living grass!

"Then, roving naked amid the stubble,
  Half a nation on hand and knee
Would worry the lawns and champ and nibble
  Or name an Institute after me."

30

Message Found in a Bottle

THROWN FROM A WINDOW AT HARKNESS PAVILION

When next upon my narrow cot,
   A prey to symptoms horrid,
I lie awake for fever's sake
   Or hold my aching forehead,
Let doctors come and doctors go,
   They'll meet with no resistance.
I'll gulp the bitterest brew. But, oh,
   Let nurses keep their distance.

For the hearts of nurses are solid gold,
But their heels are flat and their hands are cold,
And their voices lilt with a lilt that's falser
Than the smile of an exhibition waltzer.
Yes, nurses can cure you, nurses restore you,
But nurses are bound that they'll do things for you.
They make your bed up
   On flimsy excuses.
They prop your head up
   And bring you juices.
They fetch your breakfast at dawn's first crack.
They keep on pleading to rub your back.
With eau de Cologne they delight to slosh you.
And over and over they want to wash you.

The nurse-at-night you can't recall.
   She's vaguer than a dream is;
But when she whispers down the hall
   You think you're *in extremis*.

The day nurse owns a beaming face
   Designed your soul to hearten,
And speaks to you with studied grace
   As to a kindergarten.

Oh, the deeds of nurses are noble and pure,
But they're always taking your temperature.
And, dewy morn till the light grows paler,
They guard you as close as a Nazi jailer.
They pull your shades and they shut your doors.
They snub convivial visitors.
Your veriest frown
   They take to heart
And scribble it down
   On a stealthy chart.
When you reach for a smoke they're there to nab you.
With pills they dose you, with needles they jab you.
They eat the candy your friends bequeath,
And hourly urge you to brush your teeth.

The tribe of Florence Nightingale,
   Ah, let me not disparage.
How deft their ways with luncheon trays,
   How masterful their carriage!
But when the pallid look I wear
   That marks the Liquid Diet,
I wish they'd go some otherwhere
   And let me groan in quiet,
Abandoned to my germy nest,
Unnursed, unlaundered, unoppressed.

The Outcast

"Solitary reading wrong, says Adler. . . . Likens it to drinking alone."—Headlines in the *Times*.

Consider the poor sinner,
The desperate wretch by decency forsook,
Who, after dinner,
Stealthily from his shelves takes down a book
And like as not,
A drunken fool, a literary sot,
Creeps to his lonely cot,
There to swig down and out of public view
Immoderate tankards of the Pierian brew.

How sunk in vice is he! Look how he gloats,
Taking no notes,
Letting his febrile fancy roam at large in
Frivolous tomes and gay,
Despised by Mr. A.,
And annotating not a single margin.

Pity the fate
Of this inebriate.
Shunned by his fellows, none in his ear will shout
How the plot ended, how it all came out.
None in a Poetry Morning will enroll him,
No one will buttonhole him
To be an audience for some deathless prose
Recited through the nose.

But, all the precepts dead to,
Unsung at and unread to,
He'll end in squalor,
A miserable bookworm or a scholar.

The Great Enigma

I hear that Mr. Snyder now,
   Who sits in office, stately,
Has many a wrinkle in his brow
   Which was not there till lately,
From wondering how to solve aright
   This problem on his docket:
The money that is burning bright
   In everybody's pocket.
But though it's money, plain enough,
   That turns inflation's key,
What happens to the pretty stuff
   Before it gets to me?

   The money, the money,
   It's surely very funny
   What happens to the money
   Before it reaches me.

Now everyone is getting rich—
   The infant and his elder,
The digger in the union ditch,
   The merchant and the welder.
The miner climbs a golden ground,
   The jack a golden steeple,
But I don't seem to get around
   Among the proper people.

For faithful as the wolf who howls
   Along this private sector,
Beside my door, incessant, prowls
   The income-tax collector.

My salary dwindles when it's due,
  Exploding like a comet,
And every day there's something new
  To be deducted from it.

So let each bureaucratic gent
  Improve the shining hour
Inventing plans to circumvent
  The nation's buying power,
And let him study in his cell
  How best to prick the bubble,
But as for me, he might as well
  Just save himself the trouble.
For farmers live on clotted cream,
  Machinists draw their pay,
But something dams the flowing stream
  Before it comes my way.

    The money, the money,
    That makes existence sunny!
    What happens to the money
    Before it comes my way?

Memorandum for a Lynching

Have you met that original pair,
  The awf'lly amusing DeLanceys?
I must introduce you, for they're
  Brimful of the cunningest fancies.
They haven't a chick or a child,
  They haven't so much as a kitty,
But all their possessions are styled
  With titles excessively witty.
They've made it a hobby, a dear little game,
That everything's named with a whimsical name.

They live in a house that's unduly
  Bedizened with chimneys and paint,
And they call it The Mortgages. Truly!
  I think it's too utterly quaint.
The garden that blooms in its season
  Is Florence, they'll tell you with pride.
While the pool—I've forgotten the reason—
  Is Clarence, or maybe it's Clyde.
And Hiram's the fence and the elm tree is Bruno,
And True Love's the car, since it never runs—*you* know.

They'll draw your attention to Audrey, the doormat,
And Percy, the postbox,
Demure as to format.
They've happily hit on
  A name for the icebox,
The chairs that you sit on,
  The stove and the spicebox.

Your dresser is Toto, and Clara's the bed.
(It was named for an aunt who was weak in the head.)
And the sofas are called
  Esmeralda and Clancy.
Now, aren't you enthralled
  By the House of DeLancey?
You will sup
From a cup
That's referred to as Mabel.
If Leo's the clothes-lion,
Arthur's the table.
It's Jack for the bathtubs and Jill for the showers.
Oh, I could regale you for hours and hours
With tales you would simply adore. (They
  Have christened a mirror Bo Peep.)
Yes, I must introduce you before they
  Are murdered some night in their sleep.

Lesson for Ladies

"Mrs. George Pape, lady-in-waiting to Lady Tweedsmuir, was attired in dusty pink with simple diamond tiara and pearls."—*News Item.*

When next I feel inclined to grumble
    That all my hats are last year's shape,
And curse my lot and call it humble,
    I shall reflect on Mrs. Pape.

I shall remember how she went
    Amid the lords and baronesses,
With only pearls for ornament
    And simple diamonds in her tresses.

She met the curious courtiers' stare,
    She heard them whispering, "How shoddy!"
Yet never lost her casual air
    Of being good as anybody,

Nor all their laughter could embarrass
    Nor set this lady ill at ease,
Though fifty costlier tiaras
    Were bobbing to Their Majesties.

So, when my cloak of purest rabbit
    I don, and covetously think
How luckier wenches have a habit
    Of looking opulent in mink,

Or swear I'm generally fed up
    With frocks for something-ninety-nine,

I'll think of her and hold my head up,
   And wear my bargains out to dine.

Yes, Mrs. Pape I shall consider
   Braving that band of belted earls,
And flaunt them proudly as she did her
   Simple diamonds and pearls.

Song Against Sweetness and Light

How happy is the Optimist
  To whom life shows its sunny side!
His horse may lose, his ship may list,
  But he always sees the funny side.
His spirit soars on wings of hope
  And no misfortunes floor him,
But the cavalier
With views austere
  Is the man I choose before him.

The doughty Pessimist I praise.
How soothing are his quiet ways,
How comfortable are his moods,
His manners and his attitudes.
Observant that afflictions fall, he
Forbears to mar your melancholy
With admonitions most depressing
To count each individual blessing.
He does not dote on tots and nurseries.
He mourns your natal anniversaries,
And never chants with noxious glee
How the best of life is yet to be.
Nor tells you that you dwell in clover;
And he never chats till breakfast's over.

The Optimist Believes in Things
  With all his might and power.
He loves his fellow man, and sings
  Most constant in his shower.

He's cozy on a mountain height,
  Contented in a canyon,
But I insist
The Pessimist
  Is a pleasanter companion.

When Scandal rears its pretty head up,
He does not pose as being fed up
Or cry the gossiper accurst,
But handsomely believes the worst.
He does not feel his efforts hearty
Must make a go of every party.
You'd never get him to agree
The nicest things in life are free.
He scans with doubt the daily papers.
He does not laugh aside your vapors,
Or argue, reasonable, but kind,
The ailment's purely in your mind.
And though the world toward ruin roll,
He has no plan to save it whole.

O, merry is the Optimist,
  With the troops of courage leaguing.
But a dour trend
In any friend
  Is somehow less fatiguing.

Message from Mars

"Culture is necessary, but . . . not too much of it."—*Virginio Gayda, editor of the Fascist "Giornale d'Italia."*

Ah, what avails the sceptred race,
    And how shall fare that nation
Whose people know the evil face
    Of surplus education,
Where the unregimented lip
Is treasonable with scholarship?

Above that doomed, unblessèd land
    Shall hover like a vulture
The Democratic shadow and
    The nightmare shape of Culture,
While men of brawn and men of ink
Shall, likely, both aspire to think.

But here upon these happy shores
    Our ways shall never vary.
Though we admit
A little wit
    Is sometimes necessary,
We strike, before it rears erect,
The ugly head of Intellect;

And, free from erudition's taint,
    Our muscular Elite, O,
Shall strive from youth
To speak the truth
    As stated by Benito,

43

And he who follows where he's led'll
Gain the palm and win the medal.

A little language let him choose
   To read the Gospel Fascist—
A little study baiting Jew,
   Some Doctrine for the rashest,
A little War, a little Looting,
A little lesson in Saluting,
A little practice flinging down
The Bomb upon the foreign town,
A little course in shouting "Glory!"
And crying loud for Territory,
A little book-and-pamphlet burning—
But not too much of any learning.

A Model for Muddlers

General Twaddle blames "Political pressure" for keeping posts of little military value.—*Headline in the* New York Times.

Said General Twaddle,
And nodded his noddle,
"Toward ruin
We toddle;
We huddle
On Brinks.
With useless and raddled
Cantonments we're saddled,
While lawmakers, addled,
Play tiddle-
De-winks.

"Though poor Yankee Doodle's
Hell-bent for the poodles,
Like Nero
They fiddle,
When Rome
Was aflame.
Red ruin they coddle,"
Fumed General Twaddle,
"Yet idle,
We dawdle.
I call it a shame.

"Quick! Out of this muddle
Whose riddles befuddle,
Or, kit and caboodle,

In peril
We'll be.
While congressmen diddle,
Our thumbs must we twiddle?"
Cried Twaddle.
"Pish, piddle,
And fiddle-
De-dee!"

Ballad of Fine Days

Temperatures have soared to almost summer levels . . . making conditions ideal for bombing offensives.—Excerpt from B.B.C. news broadcast.

All in the summery weather,
To east and south and north,
The bombers fly together
And the fighters squire them forth.

While the lilac bursts in flower
And buttercups brim with gold,
Hour by lethal hour,
Now fiercer buds unfold.

For the storms of springtime lessen,
The meadow lures the bee,
And there blooms tonight in Essen
What bloomed in Coventry.

All in the summery weather,
Fleeter than swallows fare,
The bombers fly together
Through the innocent air.

Tactics for Offense

"An attack on the 'bad taste' of Britain's first popular war song, 'We're Going to Hang Out the Washing on the Siegfried Line,' was made in Berlin's English news broadcast."—*The New York Times*.

The German's brave as brave can be.
　　His heart beats high at war-time,
As off to meet the enemy
　　He marches in 4-4 time.
He marches north, he marches south,
　　Nor comprehends what fear is.
The taste of battle on his mouth
　　More sweet than lager beer is.
Amid the cannon's thunder-claps
　　He holds his forts and trenches.
But at an English social lapse,
　　How timidly he blenches!

For the Nordic soul is sensitive
　　And scrupulous and skittish.
The raking gun,
　　The bursting bomb,
They find him un-
　　Afraid and calm.
What really shatters
　　His aplomb
　　　Is the rudeness of the British.

Let England hang her head in shame,
　　From Devonshire to Mayfair!
Though war's a most diverting game,
　　They simply will not play fair.

48

With ballads in the worst of taste
  And quite uncivil ditties,
They lay the foeman's country waste
  And devastate his cities.
With gaucheries they undermine
  What courage takes its root on,
And send a shiver down the spine
  Of every valiant Teuton.

So call the culprit nations forth
  And pledge them to this vision:
Oh, let them plunder,
  Let them kill,
Tear towns asunder
  If they will
But guard the Aryan
  Spirit, still,
    From music-hall derision.

The Web

Oh, what a tangled web we weave
When first we practice to deceive!
Which leads me to suppose the fact is
We simply ought to get more practice.

Poor Timing

I sing Saint Valentine, his day,
  I spread abroad his rumor—
A gentleman, it's safe to say,
  Who owned a sense of humor.
Most practical of jokers, he,
  Who bade sweethearts make merry
With flowers and birds and amorous words,
  In the month of February.
The antic, frantic,
Unromantic
  Middle of February.

Now, April weather's fine and fair
  For love to get a start in.
And May abets a willing pair,
  And June you lose your heart in.
There's many a month when wooing seems
  Both suitable and proper.
But the mating call unseasonal
  Is bound to come a cropper.

When blizzards rage with might and main
  And a man's best friend's his muffler,
Pity the February swain,
  That sentimental snuffler,
Whose soul must surge, whose pulse must throb
  With passionate cadenza,
When he yearns instead for a cozy bed
  Alone with influenza.

51

When winds blow up and snow comes down
  And the whole gray world seems horrider,
And every lass that sulks in town
  Thinks wistfully of Florider,
Pity the chapped and wintry maid
  Who'd trade the arms that clasp her in,
For Vitamin A and a nasal spray
  And maybe a bottle of aspirin.

Who wants to bill, who cares to coo,
  Who longs for cherry-chopping,
When noses are red and fingers blue
  And the hemoglobin's dropping?
Let summer lovers droop and pine,
  Let springtime hearts be airy.
I wouldn't be anyone's Valentine
  In the month of February.
The spare-able, terrible,
Quite unbearable
  Middle of February.

Petition to the Postmaster-General

(TO BE SIGNED BY EVERY WOMAN WHO EVER TRIED TO MAIL A LETTER
WITH A PACKAGE UNDER HER ARM)

Lord of the loud Convention,
   Protector of the Mails,
Come lend your shrewd attention
   To my despairing wails.
I swear by public notary
   And all the heavens high,
You never had a votary
   More votive than am I.
But love's fond wings are clipt-o,
   And love's foundation rocks,
When I must stand on tiptoe
   To reach the letter box;

When I, with rising choler,
   Must grope and pant and frown,
Or beckon someone taller
   To hold the handle down,
Or blindly shift my parcels
   With many a muttered curse,
And strain my metatarsals,
   And lose my poise and purse.
My strong affection bendeth,
   And, sir, you risk my vote,
When struggle so attendeth
   The mailing of a note.

Ungrudgingly I wish you
   Success beyond debate

For stamps of every issue,
   Smooth-edged or perforate.
Your couriers, I praise them,
   As on their rounds they press.
Nor heat nor nightfall stays them,
   Nor changes of address.
But from my soap-or-better-box,
   Upon this text I preach:
Oh, put the corner letter box
   Down somewhere in my reach.

The Progress of Dictatorship

German:

The scruples of Hitler
Grow litt'ler and litt'ler.

Italian:

Beyond the Alps, as histories note,
Lies Italy and in her throat.

Russian:

Good comrades fall in
Step with Stalin.

Domestic:

Our Baby with an air imperial
Firmly declines to eat her cereal.

Go on, You Scintillate

When I am worn with witty folk,
  Fatigued by clever friends
Who see the point of every joke
  Before a story ends;
When intellects superior
  Have tired me to my bones,
I feel a strong affection for
  The Anderson B. Jones,
My heart no warmer corner owns
  For anyone to share
Than I can offer to the Jones,
  That comfortable pair.

  Ah, the Anderson Joneses, I view them with gratitude
    Age cannot wither nor custom annul.
  Their chatter is charming with bromide and platitude—
    Sweetly, wholeheartedly, cozily dull.

The Joneses hold Jehovah helps
  The ones that help themselves,
And Dr. William Lyon Phelps
  Has stocked their reading shelves.
But they are tranquil on their seat
  While other people hold forth,
Nor feel obliged to think up neat
  Allusions to be rolled forth.
They do not call a spade a spade
  In brilliant Anglo-Saxon.
Their minds are overstuffed, but made
  Expressly to relax on.

Confide them your troubles, they'll certainly pause
   To remark, when it rains how it frequently pours.
And I dote on the Anderson Joneses because
   They are precious, delightful, unmitigate bores.

They freely grant that for their part
   (And let the heavens strike)
They may not know just what is Art,
   But they do know what they like.
They never spend their afternoons
   In sharpening words to thin points,
Nor prick your private, pet balloons
   With little verbal pin points.
Their humor, though essential ham,
   Cuts less than edgèd knives,
And they've never made an epigram
   In all their blessed lives.

The Anderson Joneses to whimsy are blinded.
   They dish out clichés in deliberate tones.
They're heavy and placid and serious-minded.
   I think I'll go over and call on the Jones.

Ballad of the Lord and Columbus

Christopher Columbus, weary old tar—
  Fresh was the heavenly morning—
Came one day to the Judgment Bar,
  Roused by the trumpet's warning;
Rose up lightly, but with some surprise,
Looking around him and rubbing his eyes.
(For he'd done his share of toiling and of weeping
And the Lord had left him a long time sleeping.)

"Christopher Columbus," the Lord's voice spoke,
"You've had your slumber and it's time you woke.
The years are mounting,
  The centuries hum,
And every soul's accounting
  Is bound to come."
And He signed to Peter, nodding at His knee,
"Fetch the Final Record that is filed in 'C.' "

Columbus waited with a troubled look
While the Lord went thumbing through the Golden Book,
While the angels harped with suitable decorum
And the saints sat around in a haloed quorum
And the stars went whirling in an endless dance.
Said Christopher Columbus, "I'll take my chance.
A man's but human when he sails the seas,
But You know I stuck by my theories.
A queen had the credit and a king had the loot,
But I reached the Indies by the Western route."

Jehovah frowned and His voice was thunder.
"The sons of Adam, they are doomed to blunder.
Pitiful their follies of the future and the past,
But even My patience hath an end at last.
You steered a passage toward the setting sun—
Regard the work that your hand has done."
(Christopher Columbus felt the heavens shake.)
"Must I forgive you for this mistake?

"I was ever vext by my peopled planet.
There's always been trouble since Eve began it.
In Africa and Asia, in Albion and Spain,
Trouble and sorrow and wars and pain—
Never any quietude, never any peace
In Italy or Egypt or Palestine or Greece.
Half the world in turmoil, with woe bent double!
Yet you must go discovering a brand-new trouble."

The winds from the spheres grew shrill and loud.
    Now shivered the saints anointed.
Christopher Columbus knelt upon a cloud
    And looked where the Master pointed.
"Sailor," said the Lord, "four hundred years
This land has been a crying, a clamor in My ears,
While you lay sleeping till the Judgment Day.
Now rise and answer for the U.S.A."

From the golden pavement, from the gateway pearled,
Columbus looked on the spinning world.
He saw the mountains, and he saw the sea,
He saw America where India should be.
He saw the cities and the fields of grain,
    And he heard the voice of the Lord complain:

"Behold the things that you brought to pass:
The great towns bellowing in tones of brass;
Billboards rising where the wild deer wandered,
The earth despoiled and the forests squandered;
Men looking down where My hills used to look up;
Swing bands squealing on a national hookup;
Strikes and riots
   And bursting dams;
Hollywood diets
   And subway jams;
A thousand new religions shouting out their wares;
Floods and dust bowls and two World Fairs;
Politics and panics and boys in breadlines,
And everywhere the sound of their shrieking headlines.
The heroes dead and the giants departed.
Now rise and answer for the thing you started!"

Christopher Columbus, sturdy old tar,
Stood up straight at the Judgment Bar.
He bowed to Michael with his shining sword,
   He bowed to the Great White Throne.
Then Christopher Columbus spoke to the Lord
   In a reasonable tone:

"I saw the mountains, I saw the plain,
I saw the place where my ships had lain,
And reaching northward till time took flight,
There was America, gleaming in the light.
I heard the tumult, I heard the clamor,
The hiss of the rivet, the noise of the hammer,
The speeches and the shouting and the sound of cheers
And, Lord, it was strange to my sleep-filled ears.

60

But I saw such wonders and I heard such mirth
As I never knew when I walked on earth!

"A proud young race and their children and their sires,
Dwelling in their houses, working at their fires;
And some were weeping,
  And some were old,
And some were sleeping,
  Hungry and cold,
And some were wailing for the times askew,
But, Lord, it was better than the world I knew.

"Tanned and tall were their sons and their daughters.
They had won the valleys, they had tamed the waters.
I saw them soaring
  Through the conquered air.
Their trains went roaring
  Everywhere.
Strong their buildings and their bridges stood.
The land was fertile and the harvests good.
And a hundred million people
  Lived in brotherhood.
The Jew and the Gentile had joined their labor.
And none there feared to address his neighbor.
And there was order
  And the guns had died
Along their border,
  A continent wide.

"And freedom still on their hilltops hovered.
Lord, I have seen what my ships discovered.
Let whirlwind shake it, let lightning strike it.
I have looked on this land, and, Lord, I like it."

In the Golden City there was silence for a while.
Then the watching angels saw Jehovah smile.
And He chuckled, "There's sense in a sailor lad.
It's a noisy nation, but it's not so bad.
You rose in heaven
    And you had your say.
And you are forgiven
    For the U.S.A."

Oh, there was rejoicing on the utmost star
When Columbus came from the Judgment Bar.

II

ON THE TOWN

Dirge over a Pot of Pâté de Foie Gras

"The present chairman of the board, William A. Charles, a son of one of the founders, has no heir to carry on the name and has decided to retire. Neither is there a male heir in the family of Archibald C. Charles, which also holds an interest in the business."— *The Herald Tribune.*

Weep for an empire falling.
   Weep for a lost endeavor.
Cry ruin and woe,
Since Charles & Co.
   Has bolted its doors forever.
Let sobs be broken, let tears be saline.
Charles & Company has no male line.

Not that the Trade had left them.
   Not for a worldly reason
Are the cupboards locked
And the shelves unstocked
   With succulence out of season.
A cause more sad and a lack more germinal
Has dimmed that glory beside the Terminal.

For where are the sons of Charles's,
   Heirs to the founding sires?
Who shall be lord
Of the Governing Board
   When William A. retires?
How shall a company sell or buy on,
When feminine is its seed and scion?

The epicures keen in concert,
   The gourmet averts his glance.

65

Gone like a wind
Are the puddings, tinned,
   And the vintages out of France.
Gone the caviar, gone the truffles,
Banished by daughterly skirts and ruffles.

Gone from those splendid counters
   That watered the mouth of yore
Are the jams
And the hams
And the teas
And the cheese;
The grand things,
The canned things,
The stuffed and the potted,
The savory bits
That our wits besotted;
The soup-with-sherry,
The wild strawberry,
The bacon taken
From Cork or Kerry,
And all of the viands
That ever made merry
   Our fanciest grocery store.
Swathed are the Baskets in crepe and tissue,
For Charles & Co. has no male issue.

Incident on Madison Avenue

On Saturday, amid the crowd
  That in the sunshine drifted by,
I wandered happy as a cloud
  Afloat with fellow-cumuli,
Till suddenly, and face to face,
I came on Mr. Morgan's place.

On Mr. Morgan's house I came,
  Where wonder brought me to a standstill.
The iron gates were yet the same,
  The gardens stretched on either hand still.
But, oh, I noticed, nearly fainting,
How window sills cried out for painting.

As shabby and as weather-beat
  As those of mortgage-bearing biped,
The sashes shamed that shining street;
  They were not even washed and wipèd.
And, staring on that sight appalling,
I felt the world around me falling.

Upon my ears the tumbrels sounded,
  While wealth decayed and Fortune groaned.
I looked on Privilege, surrounded,
  The Mighty from their seats dethroned.
And quick, in terror and abasement,
I fled each drear, unpainted casement.

Now, hidden from the curious gapers,
  I weep and know the end is near.

I have not dared to read the papers,
   Lest they should tell me what I fear:
That mine and Wall Street's Patron Saint
Cannot afford a can of paint.

Sale Today

What syrup, what unusual sweet,
  Sticky and sharp and strong,
Wafting its poison through the street,
  Has lured this buzzing throng
That swarms along the counters there
  Where bargain bait is dangled—
Clustered like flies in honeyed snare,
  Shrill, cross, and well entangled?

Calendar for New Yorkers

"Only Eighty-five Days till Spring."—Newspaper adv. for a gardener's catalogue.

Vague are the days till Valentine's Day.
  Who knows the weeks till June?
While, sure day and fatal day,
Everyone's Natal Day
  Always arrives too soon.
Who counts the time till Mother's Day
  Save possibly Mr. Schling?
And months must pass
Till it's Michaelmas
  But it's eighty-five days till spring.

Eighty-five days till the houndlings bark
  Hard on the tracks of winter;
Till, tough and hopeful, in Central Park
  Emerges the grassy splinter.
Eighty-five days till the flowered hat
  Appears on the coiffured blonde,
And the buds begin, and the ice grows thin
  On the Rockefeller Pond.

Till sleep the trains that carried the ski,
  And the driver dreams at the throttle;
Till the tablets primed with Vitamin D
  Grow stale in the dusty bottle;
Eighty-five days till the shrubberies bloom
  Over the doors at Saks's,
And the postmen pound their appointed round,
  Collecting the Income Taxes.

Till couples stroll in the evening air
  And the roofs grow warm with lovers;
Till the young moth wakes in the barrel chair
  And sofas yearn for their covers;
Eighty-five days of the steam that fails
  And the pipes that knock in swing time.
Then off with the woes that winter knows,
  And on with the ills of springtime!

For long are the days till Labor Day,
  With many a moon gone by;
We've months to endure
Till Yom Kippur,
  And weeks till the Fourth of July.
It's a weary time 'til it's Christmas Time
  When progeny has its fling,
But hey nonny nonny,
The outlook is bonny.
  Just eighty-five days till spring.

Still Life

"The policy of the Association opposes the use of motion, moving objects, live models, mechanical devices, or other similar devices in window displays. . . ."—The Fifth Avenue Association.

No pinwheel, rocket, colored flare.
   No festive blizzard snowing paper.
No tricks to lure the vulgar stare
   Of idle gaper.

No elephant or pony acts.
   No cages with performing birdies.
No waterfalls, no cataracts,
   No hurdy-gurdies.

No posturing clowns with putty noses.
   No dancers, either fan or Attic.
Nothing save mannequins in poses
   Distinctly static.

Stale, flat, unprofitable the view
   Since lords of commerce, met in quorum,
Have guaranteed our Avenue
   Its strict decorum.

No bonfires, no balloons inflating.
   Not even a turnstile fit to enter.
Let's go and watch the excavating
   At Radio Center.

Lament

(UPON LEARNING THAT GROVER WHALEN IS NO LONGER LISTED AMONG
THE NATION'S BEST-DRESSED MEN)

Weep, city of boroughs and bridges,
Wail, desolate town.
To the dust, to the ants and the midges
Your grandeurs go down.
The tailors have spoken. An age that was splendid
Is ended.

That glossy perfection which blossomed more rich than the rose
From official tonneaus;
That artful ensemble which dazzled the gaping beholder—
The accurate Shoulder,
The Pocket, restrainèd but swell,
The lordly Lapel,
The fawn-colored Glove, the Cravat,
The Spat—
To oblivion slide. They have raised up the drab and the flighty
To the seats of the mighty.

Now, wardrobes expansive but menial
Depose the regalia gardenial.
The trousers whose crease was a creed
Give way to the slovenly tweed;
While the elegant topper,
The Chesterfield, fitted and proper,
Have both come a cropper.
And amateur raiment in Mass. or the middling West
Is crowned as the best.

Oh, therefore, while Dignity keens
At a blow that is crushing,
Weep! Brooklyn, Manhattan and Queens,
Especially Flushing.
Let touring celebrities heavy of head and of heart
Amid their confetti depart.
Let cameras hide in their coverts, reporters be humble,
Let cornerstones crumble.
The tailors have spoken. The glory of Grover
Is over.

Letter to the Sixth Avenue Association

(WHO PLAN TO LINE THEIR STREET WITH TREES)

Impetuous sirs, I bid you pause
   A moment e'er you make decision.
However worthy seems your cause,
   Or sweet your green, arboreal vision,

Distrust this project. Oh, beware
   The consequences here ensuing.
Or you will deck a thoroughfare
   For your undoing.

Lulled by that verdant quietude
   Under the leaves' demure enlacements,
What woman can achieve the mood
   For bargain basements?

When elm and maple boughs beguile
   With dreams of peace like Walter Pater's,
How can she charge each roaring aisle
   Or face the frantic elevators?

Lost, then, the advertisers' art
   Which showed her frocks for seven-fifty.
She'll little care if she be smart
   Or even thrifty,

But linger in the rustic shade,
   Shunning the white sale's clashing cymbals.
And what, then, shall become of Trade,
   And who will buy the wares of Gimbels?

75

Lest you should curse the sprouting twig
   And call the swaying branch a blunder,
Pause, gentlemen, before you dig
   The asphalt under.

For God can make a tree, indeed,
   To thrive on city soil or off it.
But buyers, sirs, are what you need
   To make a profit.

Country Week End, Rainy

The rain is raining all around,
   From regions moist and upper,
On field and tree and picnic ground
   Where we had planned our supper.

It rains on rivers and on roots
   With merciless abundance,
And boats, and wrung-out bathing suits,
   Which seems to me redundance.
It rains upon the tennis court
   We don't expect to get to.
According to the last report
   Tomorrow will be wet, too.

Tomorrow we will yawn the same
   While boredom dulls the eyeballs,
And play the mournful parlor game
   And drink too many highballs.

God made the singing rain to flow
   And God knows what we *will* do.
It is not raining rain, you know,
   But sinus pains and mildew.

It's raining gnat, it's raining midge,
   And drawer that sticks, and casement.
It's raining sharp remarks at bridge
   And water in the basement.

For guest, for host, it rains despair.
   Oh, hark that silver pealing!
The rain is raining everywhere,
   Including through the ceiling.

Perhaps in town it also rains
   But not as on the yokel.
Won't someone please look up the trains
   And help me catch the local?

Rebuke to Schiaparelli

(AND THE OTHER DRESSMAKERS WHO SELECT THE
WORLD'S BEST-DRESSED WOMEN)

Undoubtedly modish, the Duchess,
  The Begum is coiffured and pearled.
But I beg to deny
What the couturiers cry
That these ten fashion-ables
In slacks or in sables
  Are the stylishest ten in the world.

For I raise my glass
To as smart a lass,
  One native to our region.
She's the girl who works for Mr. Jones—
  Her name, I think, is Legion.
You know the girl who types for Jones,
  The shining one and sleek,
Who opens mail and answers phones
  For thirty-five a week.

Her hat is as right as Marina's,
  Informed as to feathers and veil.
And her gloves are as white
(Being laundered each night)
And her slippers as neat
And as trim on her feet—
  (They were five-ninety-seven on sale.)

You've seen her on the Avenue,
  Admired her on the El.
Her navy blue might shame Patou,
  Her jacket cries Chanel.
What noons to prowling given o'er,
  What raids on little shopp-es,
Have gone to keep her furbished for
  The files and carbon copies!
What matter if she stood in line
  To storm the Store-Wide Clearance;
Her topcoat may be labeled "Klein"
  But Paris, its appearance.
Her casual tweeds are British tweeds,
  Impeccable and tidy,
Though I've a hunch
They meant no lunch
  From Saturday to Frid'y.

It is simple enough to be dashing
  In wardrobes by Lelong or Worth.
But let blond baronesses
In custom-made dresses
Look well to their crowns
As the toasts of their towns
  And the nattiest ladies on earth.

For *I* state
My candidate
  Can file a prior claim.
She's secretary to Mr. Jones
  And Legion is her name.

She's urban as the paving stones,
   Miraculously chic—
That pretty girl who works for Jones
   At thirty-five a week.

Musings Aboard the Stamford Local

(DURING AN EXPEDITION INTO DARKEST WESTCHESTER)

In New Rochelle, in New Rochelle,
How placidly the people dwell
'Mid lawn and tree and fringèd gentian
And furnaces that need attention.

The sky's a blue and radiant banner
Above the roofs of Larchmont Manor,
With sun at all the curtained casements
And water frequent in the basements.

A thousand little sailboats fleck
The tides that touch Mamaroneck;
And stately houses front the Sound, too.
Mosquitoes there I think abound, too.

Oh, beautiful beyond comparison
Appear the spacious views of Harrison.
Lovely doth every vista look there.
I hear it's hard to get a cook there.

The oaks grow wide, the elms grow high
That shade the pleasant homes of Rye,
So winter-snug, so sweet in summer,
Beloved of the ardent plumber.

From urban cares that fret and fester,
Far, far away lies old Port Chester.
How much of good has life to give there!
I know some people who even live there.

Admonition in January

(ON PASSING A FLORIST'S FILLED WITH PUSSY WILLOWS)

An urban mind has learned to bear
   The calendar's perpetual treason:
Strawberries ripe for winter fare
   And skating out of season;

Shop windows of December, bold
   With swim suits daringly contrived here,
And August magazines grown old
   Ere June has half arrived here.

But pussy willows wake our dream.
   They wear a true, a springtime label,
And what necessities redeem
   This flouting of the fable?

Here, incubated and absurd,
   They droop in shivering sorority.
Their hopeful voices rise unheard
   Above the storm's authority.

And sharper seems the wind, and chill,
   With April farther off than payday,
And endless all the days until
   They have their proper heyday.

Florists, beware! Amid the snows
   Let orchids blossom for the vendor.

Permit the violet and the rose
  To thrive in hothouse splendor,

But leave these innocents to sing
An honest prophecy of spring.

Monologue in a Pet Shop

Some folks discourse
On the noble horse
  And some by newts are smitten,
While others aver
Their heartstrings stir
  At sight of a frolic kitten.
For every brute,
Though meek, though mute,
  There's somebody madly cares,
But me, I think
I'll settle for mink
  Done up by Revillon Frères.

For I am a lady with pet resistance.
Now, take the dog (and to any distance).
He's a faithful buddy
  To man, no doubt,
But his paws are muddy,
  His hair falls out.
In accents florid
  At dawn he rehearses.
His bark is horrid,
  His bite much worse is.
At little dangers
  He crawls away closer.
He follows strangers
  But nips the grocer.

You fondle, you feed him,
  You guard his habits.
And when you need him,
  He's chasing rabbits.

I lift my lute and I tune my lyre
In bold defiance of Ellin Speyer.
For cats are clawers.
  Their blood runs clammily,
In bureau drawers
  They deposit their family.
Horses are splendid
  As things to bet on,
But not intended
  For me to get on.
Goldfish stare at one,
  Calm and chilly.
Parrots swear at one,
  Monkeys act silly.
Mice I'm at bay from.
  Birds are a bore.
Pets, keep away from
  My cottage door.

It's true the acumen
Of Genus human
  Is lower than spire or steeple,
But the more I see
Of the Pekinee,
  The more I am fond of people.

III

PRIVATE AND PERSONAL

Lament for a Wavering Viewpoint

I want to be a Tory
   And with the Tories stand,
Elect and bound for glory
   With a proud, congenial band.
Or in the Leftist hallways
   I gladly would abide,
But from my youth I always
   Could see the Other Side.

How comfortable to rest with
   The safe and armored folk
Congenitally blessed with
   Opinions stout as oak!
Assured that every question
   One single answer hath,
They keep a good digestion
   And whistle in their bath.

But all my views are plastic,
   With neither form nor pride.
They stretch like new elastic
   Around the Other Side;
And I grow lean and haggard
   With searching out the taint
Of hero in the Blackguard
   Or of villain in the saint.

Ah, snug lie those that slumber
   Beneath Conviction's roof.
Their floors are sturdy lumber,

There windows weatherproof.
But I sleep cold forever
    And cold sleep all my kind,
For I was born to shiver
    In the draft from an open mind.

Why, Some of My Best Friends Are Women!

I learned in my credulous youth
  That women are shallow as fountains.
Women make lies out of truth
  And out of a molehill their mountains.
Women are giddy and vain,
  Cold-hearted or tiresomely tender;
Yet, nevertheless, I maintain
  I dote on the feminine gender.

For the female of the species may be deadlier than the male
But she can make herself a cup of coffee without reducing
The entire kitchen to a shambles.

Perverse though their taste in cravats
  Is deemed by their lords and their betters,
They know the importance of hats
  And they write you the news in their letters.
Their minds may be lighter than foam,
  Or altered in haste and in hurry,
But they seldom bring company home
  When you're warming up yesterday's curry.

And when lovely woman stoops to folly,
She does not invariably come in at four A.M.
Singing Sweet Adeline.

Oh, women are frail and they weep.
  They are recklessly given to scions.
But, wakened unduly from sleep,
  They are milder than tigers or lions.

Women hang clothes on their pegs
    Nor groan at the toil and the trouble.
Women have rather nice legs
    And chins that are guiltless of stubble.
Women are restless, uneasy to handle,
But when they are burning both ends of the scandal,
They do not insist with a vow that is votive,
How high are their minds and how noble the motive.

As shopping companions they're heroes and saints;
They meet you in tearooms nor murmur complaints;
They listen, entranced, to a list of your vapors;
At breakfast they sometimes emerge from the papers;
A Brave Little Widow's not apt to sob-story 'em,
And they keep a cool head in a grocery emporium.
Yes, I rise to defend
    The quite possible She.
For the feminine gend-
    Er is O.K. by me.

Besides everybody admits it's a Man's World.
And just look what they've done to it!

Ode to the Bath

"Dear to us ever is the banquet, and the harp, and the dance, and changes of raiment, and the warm bath, and love, and sleep."— *The Odyssey,* Book VIII.

Seven our sins are, and our virtues seven.
    Seven times ten our years' unwithered span.
And seven are the immortal mercies given
    To ease the lot of Man:
Slumber and food to keep his body whole,
    Fine raiment that proclaims his outward merit,
Motion, and music where he feeds his soul,
    And love to nurse his spirit—
These six are needful; but the seventh thing
    More constant succor hath.
Attend me, Muse, while loyally I sing
    The ancient consolation of the Bath.

Yes, haste, Pieridean daughters;
    Assist me while I praise
Those warm and living waters
    That comfort all my days.
Shunning the upstart shower,
    The cold and cursory scrub,
I celebrate the power
    That lies within the Tub.

For this alone of our enchantments seems
    Blessing without a barb.
The sleeper lies entangled in his dreams,
    The banquet ends in sodium bicarb.

The moth invades the coat, the harpers fail,
　　The dance grows dull or all the dancers bedfast,
And love itself turns weary, flat, and stale.
　　Only the Bath is steadfast,
Whose last caress is as the first embrace,
　　Where limbs repose, the burdened shoulders sink,
And the lean mind, for half an hour's space,
　　Forbears to think.

Not for the casual washer
　　On simple cleanness bent,
Not for the hasty splasher
　　Awaits the Sacrament.
Rewards are made to measure.
　　And devotees recall
That he who bathes for pleasure
　　Must keep the ritual.

With spendthrift hand lay out the towels in order,
　　Easy of access, fresh and soft as hope;
Let sponge be fluffy, but the brushes harder,
　　And lathersome the soap.
Bring out the bath salts, decorously scented
　　Of lavender or pine.
Bring pillow that the head may rest contented—
　　Then turn the tap, release the flood divine
Till it three-quarters fill the porcelain chalice,
　　Not cold or hot but tempered to desire.
And there's your refuge that was mankind's solace
　　When Homer struck his lyre.

For brighter joys may alter
　　And livelier pastimes close,

94

But in this happy shelter
    Peace blossoms like a rose.
Of all refreshments primate,
    The last Beatitude,
It keeps unchanging climate
    Where care may not intrude.
Let others, worn with living
    And living's aftermath,
Take Sleep to heal the heart's distress,
Take Love to be their comfortress,
Take Song or Food or Fancy Dress,
    But I shall take a Bath.

Nursery Rhyme

Heigh ho,
This much I know:
What they say about men
Is largely so;
What they've told about women
From Eve to Ruth
Is sober counsel,
Is gospel truth;
Tabby and Thomas
Make dubious friends.
And that's where Wisdom
Begins and ends.

Short History of Cooks

Dorcas broke the dishes,
  Clara slumbered late,
Norah's sauces
Were total losses,
  And Sigrid stole the plate.
Mabel burnt the entrées
  And wooed the handy man,
But rich and rare
And beyond compare
  Are the works of Katharine Anne.

For Katharine Anne is a cook of cooks.
She throws away the recipe books
To bake by ear or by inspiration
And her meagrest stew is a World Sensation.
She lives to nourish the urge that's inner.
She doesn't mind if there's ten to dinner.
Lighter than foam
  Is her cheese soufflé,
And she bides at home
  When it's her off day.
On her morning coffee we call a blessing,
She doesn't put sugar in salad dressing,
Her roasts should hang in a gourmet's gallery,
And she thinks that we ought to lower her salary.

Nellie was a lady
  Who kept me in my place,
Emma's seasoning
Lacked rhyme or reasoning,
  And ennui troubled Grace.

Evangelist was Idabelle
   For starchless foods and raw,
But find who can
In Katharine Anne
   A single fault or flaw.

Oh, Katharine Anne is merry and humble.
Her cakes don't fall and her pies don't crumble,
Her custards never assail us clammily,
Our larder doesn't supply her family.
The grocery bill
   Is the bill she whittles,
She lavishes skill
   On yesterday's victuals,
Her puddings gleam like a gem from Flato's,
There are no lumps in her mashed potatoes.
She's learnèd with herbs and versed in spices,
She has no sins and she owns no vices,
She likes our kitchen, she praises her bed.
And I've made her up out of my own head.

Apology for Husbands

(IN ANSWER TO A FRIEND'S OBSERVATION THAT THEY'RE
"MORE BOTHER THAN THEY'RE WORTH")

Although your major premise, dear,
   Is rather sharp than subtle,
My honest argument, I fear,
   Can offer scant rebuttal.

I grant the Husband in the Home
   Disrupts its neat machinery.
His shaving brush, his sorry comb,
   Mar tidy bathroom scenery.

When dinner's prompt upon the plate,
He labors at the office late;
Yet stay him while the stew is peppered,
He rages like a famished leopard.
He rages like an angry lion
When urged to put a formal tie on,
But should festivities grow hearty,
He is the last to leave the party.
He lauds your neighbor's giddy bonnet
But laughs, immoderate, if you don it,
And loathes your childhood friend, and always
Bestrews his garments through the hallways.

But e'er you shun the wedded male,
   Recall his special talents
For driving firm the picture nail
   And coaxing books to balance.

Regard with unalloyed delight
  That skill, which you were scorning,
For opening windows up at night
  And closing them at morning.

Though under protest, to be sure,
He weekly moves the furniture.
He layeth rugs, he fixeth sockets,
He payeth bills from both his pockets.
For invitations you decry
He furnisheth an alibi.
He jousts with taxi-men in tourney,
He guards your luggage when you journey,
And brings you news and quotes you facts
And figures out the income tax
And slaughters spiders when you daren't
And makes a very handy parent.

What gadget's useful as a spouse?
  Considering that a minute,
Confess that every proper house
  Should have a husband in it.

Comeuppance for a Progeny

"A credit of $600 may be claimed for each person . . . under
eighteen years of age."—Federal Income-Tax Report.

Arrogant girl,
  Unclasp that curl
And stifle that forward dimple.
When I swore your worth
Was the wealth of earth,
  I find I was fond and simple.
I set your price, and I set it high,
  You personal bundle from heaven, you;
But look at the market as quoted by
  The Collector of Internal Revenue!

You, our costly, our first edition,
A mine of gold to the obstetrician,
To the corner druggist whose bills unnerve us,
To Kiddie Krackers and Diaper Servus;
You, our treasure, our platinum tot,
For whom we mortgaged the house and lot,
Had better develop a sense of humor.
You're worth four hundred and not a sou more.

Cherubic tumbler,
Be meek, be humbler,
  Of tempers and tantrums, wary.
Your infant charm
May possibly warm
  The heart of the Golden Dairy.
But hushaby, baby, cease those pranks
  That harry your mom and popper.

They've got you down on the Income blanks
  At scarcely your weight in copper.

You who jingle like ready money
To him that fathered the Snuggle Bunny;
You, the original Comstock Lode
For all purveyors to our abode:
For makers of socks
  And hoods and gaiters,
Alphabet blocks
  And perambulators,
Cots and creepers
  And nursery stands,
Arnold sleepers
  And Carter bands,
Dolls and mittens
And oilcloth kittens
And christening mugs
And cribs
And bibs—
You, who rate, when the books are done,
As Luxury Item Number One,
Are here recorded beyond redemption
As four hundred dollars tax exemption.

Sold: To the Lady in the Green Hat

Some people spend their forces
   On mischievous games and crass.
Some people bet on horses,
   Some people love the glass.
But black as the pit from pole to pole,
   My destiny rideth clear,
For I am the wretch who's sold my soul
   To the Eloquent Auctioneer.

Silo,
   Flattau,
     Kaliski & Gabay!
Somewhere an auction
   Is going on today.
And I must hie me thither
   On swift, devotional feet,
To bid 'em up
On a porcelain cup
   Or a Shakespeare (Incomplete);
To beard the hardiest Dealer
   And play him fast and loose for
A screen, a rug,
Or a Staffordshire jug
   That I haven't the slightest use for.

With bureaus the attic bulges—
   With many an antique frame;
And the shallowest drawer divulges
   Statistics of my shame.

For the hart pants after the water brook,
  The novice yearns for the veil,
But never, I swear by bell and book,
  As I for the auction sale.

Plaza,
  Anderson,
    Messrs. Brill & Brill!
Somewhere an auctioneer
  Is calling high and shrill.
And I must follow, follow,
  Like the tots of Hamelin town,
To spend my sal'ry
At every gall'ry
  Where gentlemen knock 'em down.

All I need is a platter,
  All I want is a plate,
But I'll come back
With a magazine rack
  And a lamp that's lost its mate,
With maybe a chair and a couple of clocks
And a painted plaque and a music box
And a Minton bowl
And a casserole
And a lock-up cupboard without its locks.

For some people play at baccarat
  And some people tipple beer,
But mourn for the wretch, in muted verse,
Who's lost her head and pledged her purse
  To the Eloquent Auctioneer.

Much Ado About Nothing

OR

OLIVER AMES IS A DANDY

Hippety hop
To the tailor's shop,
  And summon the clothing vendor,
For Oliver Ames
This morn proclaims
  He lacks sartorial splendor.
The gray is shiny, the blue is frayed,
And far too long has he gone arrayed
In sober suitings devoutly cut on
Patterns alike to the final button.
This is the season
  Of flux and change,
Away with reason,
  Let fancy range.
While Oliver Ames, discarding navies,
Shall set more fashions than Mr. Davies.

Hurry, hurry to Tailor Scholtz.
Quick, from the shelves lift out the bolts.
Hide the serge
  With the Sunday tone!
Give him an urge
  For a herringbone.
Show him pin stripes
  And Heather-flecks,
The broad and the thin stripes,
  The plaids and checks,

Show him worsted of noble breed,
Show him cheviot, show him tweed,
Bring him everything on display
Save a classic blue or a somber gray.

And now the scissors and now the tape!
Measure and mark him, cut and drape.
Woo him with waistcoats, promise him treats
Like extra pockets and trouser pleats,
For folk must flutter and talk must stir
At the brave new wardrobe of Oliver.

Hippety hop
From the tailor shop,
   From clothier and from draper,
The suits come back
In a tidy stack
   And nestled in tissue paper.
I lift them forth. But my fingers chilly are.
These have a look that is too familiar.
The cloth is fresh and the label's new
But one is gray and the other is blue
And soberly, soberly, both are cut on
Patterns alike to the final button.
Here is the end of the toil and trouble:
He's ordered the old ones copied double.

For on this doctrine Oliver thrives:
Variety is the vice of wives.

Elegy from a Country Dooryard

When blizzards around us rejoice
    And week-enders think up excuses,
How kind seems the alien voice,
    How sweet, hospitality's uses.
But once in the summertime's clutch
    With lilies and lawns to affirm it,
I often reflect there is much
    To be said for the lot of the hermit.
For scarcely on porches and pickets
    The paint of the season is dry
But hitherward, swarming like crickets,
    The Visitors hie.

They hie here, they fly here,
    The tide never ceases.
And as they draw nigh here
    They open valises.
By steamer, by clipper,
    By train they arrive here.
Youth, granny and nipper,
    They walk or they drive here
To share in our rations
    Or stay for a night
And some are relations
    (Though some we invite).

They haste for a glimpse of the heir.
    En route to conventions they stop in.
Or dustily bound for the Fair
    They feel it their duty to drop in.

As gaily as amorous larks
   They bring us their brides when they marry.
They pause on their way to the Parks.
   Returning from seashores they tarry.
We never sit down to our pottage,
   We never go calm to our rest,
But lo! at the door of our cottage,
   The knock of the Guest.

Oh, look to the plumbing
   And bring down the cots.
The Campbells are coming
   And so are the Potts.
The cook's given notice,
   The car's on vacation,
But dear cousin Otis
   Just phoned from the station.
It's dear Otis, is it?
   Well, tell him, the elf,
I've gone on a visit
   To someone myself.

Song for an Engraved Invitation

Now, warm and sweet, the summer days
   Are opening like the rose,
With drowsy airs and languid ways
   Inviting to repose.
But not for me a green retreat
   Or any vernal asset,
Since up and down the panting street
   I stalk the demitasse set,
Or trail the silver berry spoon,
   While lunch I dare not stop for.
For what's so rare as a day in June
   Without a gift to shop for?

O June, fair June, what a month you are—
The costliest time in the calendar!
Filled, as a nettle is full of stings,
With sweet occasions for giving things.

Wherever I look, whenever I listen,
Solitaires gleam and diplomas glisten
Or babes from darkness
Emerge at Harkness
Or somebody's child is ripe to christen
Or somebody's daughter is taking a spouse
Or somebody's warming a country house
Or somebody's fledgling has finished the tenses
At Taft or Groton or maybe Spence's.

December giving strains the purse,
  December lists are grievesome.
Still, Christmas presents might be worse—
  You're certain to receive some.
But when I scurry far and wide
  Or fevered errands fly on
In search of plates to please a bride
  Or mugs to suit a scion,
I know full well that I must brood
  For solace through the summer
On pretty notes of gratitude
  And a whacking bill from Plummer.

Sailings and weddings and births and showers!
My fate is sealed for the month of flowers.
When the first June wind blows soft and south,
I'll be looking a gift shop in the mouth.

A Hobby a Day Keeps the Doldrums Away

OR

THE PROJECTS OF OLIVER AMES

This is Oliver's garden . . .
Here is the earth we watched him splinter
When spring was baying the tracks of winter.
Here are the bountiful beds he laid out
The earliest day he could get his spade out.
These are his borders—you couldn't miss 'em—
Of ageratum and sweet alyssum.
These are the plots where he put his signs up,
Yonder his trellis to lure the vines up,
And here are the flowers he let go *their* ways
When "Fore" resounded along the fairways;
The blooms I reared in the sweat of my brow.
For it's *my* garden now.

This is Oliver's workshop . . .
Behold the nook where my hero planned to
Build whatever he set his hand to.
Observe his hammers and saws and wrenches,
His braces and bits, his drawers and benches.
These are his cupboards—a costly come-on.
This is the tool that he cut his thumb on,
And here is the table he almost finished
Before his masculine zeal diminished,
When he decided perhaps he might
Leave some of the laurels for Hepplewhite;
While here are the cobwebs that coil and cluster
For *my* broom and duster.

Sing hey for Oliver's playthings . . .

For the wireless set that he cannot send with,
For the tropical fish that I contend with,
For the herbs I hang when he tires of cookery,
For the books I shelve in his unread bookery,
For the faithful hound of a doting master
That I take out to avoid disaster;
The trays and acids in which I traffic
When palls the interlude photographic;
The grain he buys for the snowbound starlings
That I distribute—they're all my darling's.
Each for the moment his one, his true love,
And mine to store when he takes a new love.

For Man proposes the Fuller Life,
But the debris's disposed of by his wife.

Millinery Memo

I can keep a fairly reasonable attitude
Toward the snood.

But even the girl with long eyelashes and a dimple
Looks pretty simple
In a wimple.

Twelfth Night

Down from the window take the withered holly.
Feed the torn tissue to the literal blaze.
Now, now at last are come the melancholy
Anticlimactic days.

Here in the light of morning, hard, unvarnished,
Let us with haste dismantle the tired tree
Of ornaments a trifle chipped and tarnished.
Pretend we do not see

How all the room seems shabbier and meaner
And all the house a little less than snug.
Fold up the tinsel. Run the vacuum cleaner
Over the littered rug.

Nothing is left. The postman passes by, now,
Bearing no gifts, no kind or seasonal word.
The icebox yields no wing, no nibbled thigh, now,
From any festive bird.

Sharp in the streets the north wind plagues its betters,
While Christmas snow to gutters is consigned.
Nothing remains except the thank-you letters,
Most tedious to the mind,

And the bright gadget which must wait no longer
To be exchanged (by stealth) at Lewis & Conger.

Well, Well, Charlie's in Town

OR

THE FRIENDS OF OLIVER AMES

When I was wed to Oliver
  We swore eternal ties,
And the marriage vows
Can still arouse
  My sentimental sighs.
His lot my very lot shall be,
  But somewhere courage ends.
For I'll embrace his destiny,
  But not his bachelor friends.

Find me a burrow! Hide me fast.
Here comes Oliver's Awful Past.
Here come the lads he reveled late with
Ere I was the one he cast his fate with,
The boon companions, the props and stays
That comforted him in his single days.

Look! Here's Herbert, the human blotter,
(And Herb was a card at alma mater)
Who'll drink our liquor and leave us iceless,
Recalling the pranks that were Simply Priceless.

Lock up the chinaware. Here comes Mac,
A demon shot with the bric-a-brac.
Indoor games are his favorite pastime.
(My Dresden vase was the target last time.)

Here comes Artie—he calls me "Missis"—
And Fred, who gallantly reminisces
Of madcap Margies and matchless Claires
Who figured once in my lord's affairs.

Way for the comrades he knew of old,
The Salt of the Earth, the Hearts of Gold,
Who fly from Cleveland or rush from Reno
To drag us forth to the French Casino,
Who fill our ash trays and share our meals
And borrow ten till they Close those Deals.

In health as in the common cold
  My lawful spouse I cherish.
Through plump and slim
I cleave to him,
  Through markets dull or bearish.
My fondest hopes, my dearest joys
  In Oliver are carried.
But save me from the Rover Boys
  He knew before we married.

Inventors, Keep Away from My Door

Ah, where's the patented device
  That I can learn to master?
My icebox yields me melted ice,
  My oven, but disaster.
From stranded cars it is my fate
  To view the rural scenery;
For I'm the poor unfortunate
  Undone by all machinery.

Other people's robots keep a willing head up.
  All their cheerful keyholes welcome in the key.
Other people's toasters do not burn their bread up.
  But nothing ever works for me.

The gadgets come, the gadgets go,
  Ambitious for the attic.
Tune up my stubborn radio—
  It screams with rage and static.
The vacuum sweeper roundabout
  With slippery strength encoils me.
Locks treacherously lock me out.
  The simple corkscrew foils me.

Other people's mousetraps sometimes bring a mouse down.
  Other people's furnaces sing in cozy glee.
Mine huffs and it puffs till it brings the quaking house down.
  Nothing ever runs for me.

The humblest tools in my abode
  Know half a hundred ruses

To leak or sputter or explode,
  Catch fire or short their fuses.
In all things made of steel or wire,
  Inanimate, unholy,
There lurks some dark, ancestral ire
  Directed at me, solely;
There lurks some black, malicious spite
  Amid the wheels and prisms,
And what shall save me from the might
  Of wrathful mechanisms?

Other people's watches do not send them late for
  Amorous appointment or literary tea.
Other people's telephones bring the word they wait for.
  But *nothing* ever works for me.

The Female of the Species Is Hardier Than the Male

OR

THE INCONSISTENCY OF OLIVER AMES

Oliver Ames is a stalwart man,
  Whose strength is a gushing fountain.
With a nonchalant smile he swims his mile
  Or conquers the savage mountain.
Girded for sport, he holds the fort
  When rivals are round him dropping.
But clear the deck
For a Total Wreck
  Whenever I take him shopping.

Oliver is winded, Oliver's awry.
He clutches at the counters and he plucks at his tie.
On his overheated face
  There's a weary sort of frown,
And he's looking for a place
  Where he can just sit down.
And he mops at his forehead
  And he tugs at his cuff,
And in language terse and torrid
  He swears he's had enough.

Now, a sturdy oak is Oliver Ames,
  While I am the ivy, twining.
I make no claims for my skill at games
  And I exercise best, reclining.
But when I'm out on a shopping bout
  Where the glittering price tags leer up,

Stouter and bolder,
It's always my shoulder
   That bolsters my frazzled dear up.

Saturday is young yet; I'm going like a breeze.
But Oliver is glassy-eyed and sagging at the knees.
We've only looked at draperies,
   We've only stormed the lifts
For silverware and naperies
   And half a dozen gifts;
We've only searched the basements
   For underwear and rugs
And curtains for our casements,
   And copper water jugs
And clocks and lamps and tables and blankets for the bed,
And sweater suits and neckties and a spool of cotton thread.

And still the time is ample
   For doing this and that.
I want to match a sample,
   I want to buy a hat.
I want to see the furniture that decks the Model House.
But Oliver is muttering the mutters of a spouse,
And his temper goes a-soaring
   While his metatarsals sink,
And he totters homeward, roaring
   For a pillow and a drink.

Oh, Delilah might have saved herself that legendary cropping
If she'd only taken Samson on a Saturday of shopping.

Lines from a Porch Swing

Maud Muller on a summer's day
Industriously raked the hay.
But I can think of nothing duller
Than aping the ambitious Muller.
I'll bet my hat against your jerkin
That summer was not made to work in.

Now sleeps the cloud; the skies are hazy;
Beast, bird and bee turn plump and lazy.
The grass its growing idly slows up;
The wind is languid when it blows up.
And who are we that we should try
To put to shame the grass and sky?

Travel Song with a Faint Hint of Nostalgia

For fleetness I give you the Plane
  Whose winging is swifter than words are.
It turns up its nose at terrain,
  And it flies through the air where the birds are.
Aloof from the dust and the crowd,
  Aloft in the sky, it can fly away,
Over hill, over field, over cloud,
  To China or Sioux City, Ioway.
With speed, unsurpassable, lyrical,
  It can whisk you to Bali and back.
So I give you the century's miracle,
  If you'll give *me* the Train on the Track.

It's the Old-Fashioned Train
  That I beg you bequeath me.
For I'd
Rather ride
  With the ground just beneath me,
Where the air doesn't sag
And no passenger toys with
A brown paper bag
  To recover his poise with.

The pundits in chorus agree
  There is nothing that's safer or finer,
When daring the turbulent sea,
  Than a Ship. Say a yacht or a liner.
And if you abandon the wave,
  I commend you the Auto for service—

A plaything, a tool and a slave,
  Suave, useful, ubiquitous, nervous.
But maladies heckle a motorcar,
  And the ocean has motion, alack!
So I'll give you your choice of a *boat* or car,
  And I'll take the Train on the Track.

Yes, I'll take the Old-Fashioned
  Train, if you please,
As it sails
Down the rails
  With the greatest of ease.
For the Chant of the Steel
  Is the song I insist on—
Of engine and wheel
  And the proud-pushing piston.

The smell of the cinder,
  The nocturnal tossing,
The swerve at the curve
  And the toot at the crossing,
The hum of the Diesel,
  Or hiss of the steam—
It's the Train on the Track
  That devours my dream.

The Chosen People

The brunt [of the new tax] will be borne by the middle brackets.
—*News item from the* New York Times.

I'm a middle-bracket person with a middle-bracket spouse
And we live together gaily in a middle-bracket house.
We've a fair-to-middling family; we take the middle view;
So we're manna sent from heaven to Internal Revenue.

We're the pride of every sector.
We're the darlings of the land.
To the income-tax collector
We extend a helping hand.
For the poor have empty pockets
And the rich bewail the Day,
But the middle-bracket patriots
Are steady with their pay.

When there's duty to accomplish, it's our duty that we do.
Though the world is in a muddle, we contrive to muddle
through.
We are first in all the battles as we're first in every peace,
And we lead the van devoutly when the levies must increase.

The upper brackets, nightly,
Have dreams of What's Beyond,
And to their bosoms tightly
They clutch the taxless bond.
The cheerful lower brackets
Get coupons from the gov.,
But the people in the middle
Own the legislature's love.

Oh, we reimburse the dentist and we meet the butcher bills.
We're the folks who keep the temples up, along the templed
   hills.
We are sturdy as to shoulder and our collars all are white.
So the income-tax department keeps us forming to the right.

> Then sing a song of sixpence
>   And ninety billions more.
> Hum a ballad for the wolf
>   That hangs about the door.
> But chant a pretty ditty
>   Until the welkin rings
> For the middle-bracket citizens
>   Who bear the brunt of things.

The Lass with the Monday Air

Now what's that thunder upon the stair?
It's Susan wearing her Monday Air.
She gave a slip and she gave a slide
And she climbed from her crib on the Monday side.
And the sun may shine
  Or the rain may patter,
But dreary or fine,
  It doesn't matter.
The household quivers from floor to ceiling
When Susan wakes with that Monday feeling.

Everything's spiteful, everything's horrid,
The floor jumps up and attacks her forehead.
The buildings fall that she built with blocks.
Somebody's broken the music box.
Her playthings creep
  To a distant corner.
She hates Bo Peep
  And she loathes Jack Horner.
Pins stick into her, highchairs pinch,
And cereal's awful and so is spin'ch.
The washable lamb deserts her lap,
And who in the world thought up the Nap?

Oh, childhood's garden is weeds and stubble
On Indigo Monday, day of trouble.

But what's this light in a gloomy place?
It's Susan wearing her Wednesday face.
For the crib was cozy, the crib was wide,
And Susan got up on the Wednesday side.

Let raindrops splatter,
  Or sun hold sway.
What does it matter?
  It's a lovely day.
There's music now from the nursery shelf,
And she helps to tie up her shoes herself.

Nothing is horrid, nothing is spiteful.
She thinks her parents are too delightful.
The lamb says "Susan" with happy bleating.
The oilcloth elephant nods a greeting.
The camel joyfully humps his hump
And the floor desists from the tiniest bump.
The story books keep
  Her affections whole.
She loves Bo Peep,
  She adores King Cole.
Carrots for lunch? Well, it's immaterial.
Spinach is splendid, and so is cereal.
Her toys reside in their proper haunts
And a Nap is exactly the thing she wants.

Oh, obdurate days, I give you warning:
Be Wednesday for Susan every morning.

Song for a Brand-New House

Our little home is finished,
  A dream that came to birth.
Before our eyes we saw it rise
  Upon our private earth.
Unpack the tufted rocker,
  And lay the carpets prone,
For the gilt is on our knocker
  And the neighbors on our phone.

What if plumbers in bathrooms lurk, yet,
What if the furnace doesn't work, yet,
If floors are a tint that I didn't pass on,
If someone's forgotten to turn the gas on?
If we have no shades for the bedroom casement,
If water stands in the waterproof basement,
If the drains don't drain and the windows stick
And the mantel's tile when we planned on brick?
Hang the pictures. Let life begin!
The painters are out and we are in.

No more the hired apartment,
  No more the rented lair,
With a landlord chap to take the rap
  When something needs repair.
For now, with pleasure reeling,
  Our legal nest we view,
Complete with sill and ceiling
  And a mortgage shiny-new.

Isn't it cute? It's all our own,
Save what belongs to the Building-and-Loan.

These steadfast walls with their clapboards quaint
Are ours to cherish with love and paint.
Our own the rooftree above us bending,
And ours the cost when it cries for mending.
These rooms are ours and the halls that meet them,
Likewise the fuel that it takes to heat them.
All ours, each closet and cunning feature,
While the wolf at the door is our personal creature.

Behold our dwelling, the spirit's axis.
God bless it and help us to meet the taxes!

Please Lock the Hardware Store

THE TEMPTATIONS OF OLIVER AMES

Light a light for the prodigal,
  Prepare the sternest measures.
For Oliver Ames, my all-in-all,
  Slinks home from primrose pleasures.
His gait grown loose,
  His wits unstrung,
And the glib excuse
  On his busy tongue,
Oliver's stumbling home tonight,
  While the candle sears its socket,
With the hangdog air that spendthrifts wear,
  And gadgets in his pocket.

For every man has his personal vice
  And the hardiest male his weakness.
They guess the market or fling the dice
  Or pin their hopes to the Preakness.
But it isn't the nag on
  The track beyond,
And not the flagon,
  And never the blonde
That stirs the pulse of Oliver Ames
  Till he cometh a daily cropper.
It's the sliding rule or the gardener's tool
  Or the guaranteed bottle stopper.

The little toy clock is covered with dust
  Like the patented cocktail mixer.

And the Coffeelator is red with rust
  That brewed such an odd elixir.
Now sleeps, forgot-
  Ten, the creakless hinge
That Oliver bought
  On a gadget binge.
The waxers, the glazers,
  The safety fuses,
The bladeless razors
  He never uses,
The strange utensils
  For spading grass up,
The streamlined pencils
  He couldn't pass up,
Collapsible trinkets or automatic,
They clutter the cupboards, they fill the attic.
But Oliver's shambling home again
  From paying his private piper,
With a portable stand
In his shaking hand,
  Or a chromium windshield wiper.

For a thirstier soul may crave the bowl
  Till he'll borrow or beg or cadge it,
And the moth's fair game for a candle flame,
  But Oliver loves a gadget.

Notes for a Southern Road Map

Carry me back to old Virginny,
    Land of cotton and the Williamsburg Plan,
Where the banjo calls to the pickaninny
    And the sun never sets on the Ku Klux Klan.
Carry me anywhere south of the line, there,
    To old Kentucky or Fla. or Tenn.,
But when I hear that it's time to dine, there,
    You can carry me North again.
For Dixie's myth is a myth I dote on;
    The South's my mammy is what I mean.
But never, ah never, they'll get my vote on

    Their pet cuisine.
For it's ham,
Ham,
Frizzled or fried,
Baked or toasted,
Or on the side.
Ham for breakfast
And ham for luncheon,
Nothing but ham to sup or munch on.
Ham for dinner and ham for tea,
Ham from Atlanta
To the sea,
With world-worn chicken for change of venue,
But ham immutable on the menu.

Dear to my heart are the Southland's bounties,
   Where honeysuckle is sweet in May,
Where warble the Byrds from important counties
   And everything runs by the TVA.
I love the mint that they spice the cup with,
   Their women fair and their horses fast;
An accent, even, can I put up with,
   And stories, suh, from a Noble Past.
So carry me back to an old plantation
   In North Carolina or Alabam',
But succor me still from a steadfast ration
   Of ham.

Ham,
Ham,
Not lamb or bacon
But ham in Raleigh
And ham in Macon.
Ham for plutocrats,
Ham for pore folk,
Ham in Paducah and ham in Norfolk;
In Memphis, ham, and in Chapel Hill,
Chattanooga,
And Charlottesville.
Ham for the Missy,
Ham for the Colonel,
And for the traveler, Ham Eternal.

Oh, patriotically, I implore,
Look away, Dixieland, from the smokehouse door.

Verses for a Greeting Card

How often and how sweetly wends
This fancy toward my distant friends.

No knife can cut our love in twain
So long as distant they remain.

Humblesse Oblige

A thousand songs have toasted
  The joys of high cuisine;
Full many a bard has boasted
  Of salads, spiced and green.
They've praised the winking tumbler,
  The vine, the corn, the oil,
But I would hymn a humbler
  Devising of the soil.
While gourmets raise an eyebrow
  And quote a line from Plato,
I sing for those less highbrow
  Who love the dear Potato.

Oh, succulent, luscious, caloric and hot,
I give you Potato, the Queen of the Pot.
Though apples may comfort and flagons can stay me,
To stalwart Potato I sing my do-re-mi.

Now Beet's a ruddy fellow
  And pleasant to the tongue.
I like the wholesome yellow
  Of squash, demure and young.
Convivial companion
  Is Pea with Carrot met,
While strongly is the Onion
  Within my favor set.
And Broccoli's the winner
  Of many a toothsome race,
But ah, I rue that dinner
  Potato does not grace.

Cry shame on the lout with digestion unplacid
Who damns it for starch and dissects it for acid,
Who nibbles a Lettuce or chews on his roughage,
Complaining Potato adds poundage and puffage.

His Spinach let him munch on
    In penance for his sins,
Or make a meager lunch on
    Exclusive vitamins;
But brave and bold and fearless,
    My appetite at edge,
I'll dine upon this peerless,
    Inimitable veg.
With predatory mutter,
    I'll try the Frys of Home,
Or garnish them with butter
    And beat them light as foam.

I'll bake them in their jackets,
    I'll boil them in the nude,
I'll watch them toss in creamy sauce
    With parsleyed attitude;
I loudly shall acclaim them
    More dear than beer and skittles,
And let who will go take his fill
    Of dietary vittles.

IV

A TROUBLED POOL

Notes for an Anthropologist

Eager to get but loath to give,
A seeker and acquisitive,
A niggard born, a miser clearly,
Man as Collector ripens early,
His acts being seven ages.

                              First,
The urchin who, with forehead pursed
And eyes that wear the squirrel look,
Hoards five round pebbles from the brook.
The ten-year-oldster learns at camp
To prize the cancelled postage stamp,
While, newly shaved, the youth encumbers
His mind and cuff with telephone numbers.

Once come to man's entailed estate,
The fever grows, for early and late
He breaks his rest and wilts his collar,
Seeking the rare, the minted dollar.
And he grows frantically fond,
At fifty, of the untaxed bond.

Sixty puts on a childhood fashion
And, still the squirrel, resumes his passion
For stamps (or, if of means like Croesus',
For dubious Flemish masterpieces).

Not even age annuls the surge
Of this obscure but primal urge.

The dotard guards his shallow breath
As if it were rubies. Only death
Outwits him, when with cool affection
Earth adds him to her own collection.

Old Rhyme

Loudly while the bombs rain down
Ring the bells of London Town.

Watch out below
Cries the great bell at Bow.

You make a fine target
Say the bells of St. Marg'et.

The horsemen ride palely
Call the bells of Old Bailey.

No shelter for miles
Warn the bells of St. Giles'.

Both poor men and rich,
Toll the bells at Fleetditch,

With horror must grapple
Ring the bells at Whitechapel.

Flee fast as you can,
Shriek the bells of St. Ann,

The planes are still fleeter,
Mourn the bells of St. Peter.

There's blood in the dawn
Say the bells of St. John.

The Old Woman with Four Sons

I have had four sons, said the old woman,
And no daughter ever.
My sons are kind men, they are kinder than common,
And tall, and clever.

They come often to visit me from the places where they live,
Restless as birds.
Their hands are full of the gifts that men like to give.
Their words are men's words.

They say to me, "You are looking well," "Do you need money?",
      "The job is fine."
They chat with the neighbors.
The minds I shaped once are shaped now to a new design
By their wives or their labors.

They never come to my room at night, combing their hair,
When we are alone,
To share with me the secrets that women share
In heart and bone.

Sons do not need you. They are always out of your reach,
Walking strange waters.
Their mouths are not made for small and intimate speech
Like the speech of daughters.

The lads I bore are my sons still, said the old woman,
Grown clever and tall.
And they are kind. Oh, they are kinder than common.
But I have no daughter at all.

Address to the Younger Generation

"Children want facts, not fiction, in their reading."—Excerpt from
American Library Survey Report.

And is it truth you want, and doings factual?
    Then from the shelves take down these volumes first.
Here are your heroes. These are real and actual.
    These will assuage your thirst.

Turn from the spurious air your elders thrive in
    To this more shrewd and honest atmosphere:
The literal world that Mowgli was alive in,
    Where Robin slew the deer.

Your minds are tough, my loves, and with compliance
    Can bear the truth. So see you get it learned,
How there are ghosts and dragons, yes, and giants,
    And frogs to princes turned.

Learn about mermaids, winds among the willows,
    Knights, gnomes and monsters; read of the shepherd boy
Who fled with Helen over the wine-dark billows
    And brought the ships to Troy.

These are the verities, and you are able
    To comprehend them. Leave your elders with
Their ever-changing scientific fable,
    Their blind, Utopian myth.

Leave them their legends built on creeds and isms,
    Allow them their political fairy tales

Spun out of conquests, wars and cataclysms,
  And not-too-holy Grails.

While you, enlightened tots, shall sip the chalice
  Of perfect knowledge as your peers demand,
And keep thereby the sanity of Alice
  Roaming in Wonderland.

On Every Front

Sickened by sounds of war and pillage,
  Wearied by rumors on the air
Of stricken town and wasted village
  And death and battle everywhere,
I fled the house that horror grew in,
I fled the wireless shouting ruin,
To walk alone, a hopeful comer,
In my green garden, ripe with summer.

I leaned my head above the rose
And while I watched, her natural foes—
Beetle and slug—in barbarous fettle,
Crept to consume her, leaf and petal.
I saw the ants amid the grass
In foraging battalions pass,
Driving toward their disputed goal
For loot and *Lebensraum*. The mole,
Devious, secret, like a virus,
Bored from within upon the iris.

In captured trees had flung their tents
The caterpillar regiments.
Snails went in armor, scared and chilly,
While forward moved upon the lily
The cutthroat worm; but not for long.
Checking his desultory song,
A robin pulled the raider back
With one swift aerial attack,
But to be routed in disorder
By Tabby, pouncing from a border.

In bloody dust those armies weltered.
  Horde marched upon belligerent horde.
It was not peace my garden sheltered
  But the insatiable sword.
And watching there, I sighed. But soon,
On that same summer afternoon,
I took up arms and, stoutly met,
Slew twenty slugs with no regret.

Young Man with an Heir

From what majestic portals,
  From what Olympian ways,
You fix on common mortals
  Your condescending gaze,
Who—entering the nursery
  And halting at the door—
Have in one moment cursory
  Become an Ancestor.

This infant, red and slumbering,
  That you've so lately met—
This morsel now encumbering
  Crib, scales, or bassinet—
In him I watch you test your
  Resemblance and your mark
And straightway don the vesture
  That robes a Patriarch.

Even as you were bending
  Above your scion, now,
I saw the crown descending
  To your astonished brow.
And on your shaven chin, sir,
  I noticed as I peered,
Indubitably begin, sir,
  A faint, ancestral beard.

Before your startled stare looms
  What venerable reward!
Your chattels all turn heirlooms,
  Yourself a Foundling Lord.

And, seeing your look engravèd
  On one pink, new-born lamb,
You range yourself with David,
  Solomon, Abraham.

Portrait

I

This was her fault: that she should speak too clearly
The candid shapings of her quiet mind;
That she should carve the marble phrase too nearly
The image of her thought; that she should find
No mystery in speech, no desperate striving—
But only words obedient as bees,
As forest-bees, that know the time of hiving
And fly together to the honey-trees.

Not ever had she leaned with broken net
To catch the little colored fish that darted,
Silver and gold and amethyst and jet,
About a troubled pool, nor heavy-hearted,
Seined up a jaded few and lost the rest—
The fleet, the beautiful, the unexpressed.

II

This was her sorrow: that she comprehended
Only the broad sun and the truthful day.
Time ceased for her that hour the light was ended,
And dusk fell, and the children stopped their play.
When, in the West, the shadows were assembled,
She could not walk unfaltering any more;
A blindness came upon her, so she trembled
And went into her house and shut the door.

Never for her the headlong, laughing flight
Down any path the moon's eye might discover;

Never for her to walk the windy night,
Hand in his hand who might have been her lover.
In dark she stumbled. So she kept her room.
This was her sorrow and became her doom.

Mr. Browning Revises—1940

Oh, to be in England,
Now that April's there!
For whoever wakes in England
Sees the Placards in the square,
And workmen planting the garden closes
With bomb-proof shelters instead of roses,
While the gas-mask's tailored to suit the brow
In England, now.

And after April, when May follows,
How lads will train in the country hollows!
Look—where we used to pluck the daffodil,
They're laying out a Rural Safety Station
(Dug like a trench below the grassy hill)
Designed for London's quick evacuation
Some evening when a Siren, through the hush,
Calls louder than the thrush.
And where the hedgerows glisten in the sun
Now shyly lurks the anti-aircraft gun
Waiting to flower, when it gets its focus,
With blossoms brighter far than any crocus.

Intimations of Mortality

(ON BEING TOLD BY THE DENTIST THAT "THIS WILL BE OVER SOON")

Indeed, it will soon be over, I shall be done
    With the querulous drill, the forceps, the clove-smelling cotton.
I can go forth into fresher air, into sun,
    This narrow anguish forgotten.

In twenty minutes or forty or half an hour,
    I shall be easy, and proud of my hard-got gold.
But your apple of comfort is eaten by worms, and sour.
    Your consolation is cold.

This will not last, and the day will be pleasant after.
    I'll dine tonight with a witty and favorite friend.
No doubt tomorrow I shall rinse my mouth with laughter.
    And also that will end.

The handful of time that I am charily granted
    Will likewise pass, to oblivion duly apprenticed.
Summer will blossom and autumn be faintly enchanted.
    Then time for the grave, or the dentist.

Because you are shrewd, my man, and your hand is clever,
    You must not believe your words have a charm to spell me.
There was never a half of an hour that lasted forever.
    Be quiet. You need not tell me.

Date Due